More Psychology In Plain English

Dr. Dean Richards
Illustrated by Rebecca Richards

ISBN: 1479168416
ISBN-978-1479168415

For my wife Andrea, and our
children Matt, Ben, and Rebecca,
sources of most of my practical
experience in psychology as well
as my motivation for most of what
I do.

CONTENTS

Chapter 1: Freudian Hangovers: Scapegoating, Repressed Memory, and Dream Analysis

Dreams are often most profound when they seem the most crazy. Sigmund Freud

That all the material composing the content of a dream is somehow derived from experience, that it is reproduced or remembered in the dream- this at least may be accepted as an incontestable fact. Yet it would be wrong to assume that such a connection between the dream-content and reality will be easily obvious from a comparison between the two. On the contrary, the connection must be carefully sought, and in quite a number of cases it may for a long while elude discovery. Sigmund Freud, *The Interpretation of Dreams*

When I first moved to Southern California, I went to a number of touristy sites with various relatives and friends. At one, we were accosted by a caricature artist who proceeded to ask us what each of us did for a living, then drew pictures of each of us on the job. I made the mistake of saying I was a psychology professor. The artist must have interpreted this as "psychologist," because, in response he drew on the typical stereotype—a prototypical analyst bearing a caricature of my homely face, holding a notebook, tapping a pencil on the side of that face, and asking the patient on the couch, "So. Why do you hate your mother?"

We can all credit, or blame, Sigmund Freud for that familiar bit of cultural dogma. Though it's been 70-plus years since that bearded Viennese cigar addict met his final appointment, because of Freud, many people still believe that we're all victims of our rearing, especially victims of our mothers' actions. Many people also believe that we suffer from repressed traumas from our childhoods, and they blame those repressed traumas for our current problems. These folks will cite a whole litany of childish complaints for why they can't find true happiness now. "My mother didn't breast feed me!" "My mother didn't listen to me when I was right about something!" "My father shut my finger in the car door and told me to stop whining about it afterward even though it hurt!" "My father never said he loved me, he was always working, and he didn't listen to me when I was really scared of the monster in the closet!" "My mother never appreciated me!" Some folks even think that there may even lurk, deep within their minds, something more sinister—memory of some long buried, profound, deeply disturbing trauma. Such traumas are said to be so upsetting that we can't even retrieve them at all, a phenomenon referred to by psychoanalysts as "repressed memory." Those repressed memories of long ago are then blamed for why we currently suffer from anxiety and depression.

It's an attractive idea, this Freudian supposition that our depression, our anxiety, our inertia, or our sense of angst is not our fault, and instead is due to buried and repressed trauma. One of the things that makes the idea so popular is the scapegoating that it allows. You can convince yourself that your misery isn't your fault. You're an innocent child victim of past mistreatment. You may not know who is to blame, because the memory is repressed, but rest assured, the fault isn't yours.

Go to a slasher movie, or a movie about a psychopathic killer. Toward the end, there will always be the explanatory sequence, where we go back to the person's childhood and witness the traumatic events that led, inexorably, to the place we are now. Yes, deep in this person's childhood, there was that important, formative moment, where a traumatic event, an event long repressed, led a previously sweet, innocent child inexorably down the path to this current, bloody debacle. The killer himself (it's pretty much always a male) is tortured by the fact he doesn't understand himself. Unconscious forces drive him to kill, and he's haunted by something that he can't understand and can't put his fingers on. He kills, and kills, but he never understands why he's killing.

(Actually, the motivation of the killer in slasher movies isn't the biggest mystery that I've found in such stories. The bigger mystery is why, once the future victims of the psycho killer suspect that there's an evil maniac out there somewhere, they immediately decide to divide their forces and go exploring in widely separated directions. "Hey, something evil is trying to kill us all in a horrible, grisly fashion one at a time!" "Oh, let's split up, then, and each go into the darkest, most unprotected places we can find rather than staying here where we have light and can watch each other's backs!" "Great idea! I'll go this way, and you go somewhere else!")

The killers in the slasher movies also suffer dreams—tortured dreams that they can't understand and can't escape, dreams that offer subtle hints to the original trauma. The successful analysis of those dreams might be our killer's salvation, if only he could see past the repressed memory that's inspiring the dreams. Freud saw great significance in dreams, and he considered his dream analysis work to be his most significant achievement. He wasn't the first person to analyze dreams, of course. We all dream, and the practice of trying to make sense out of dreams goes farther back than human recorded history, probably as far back as the language needed to communicate about dreams. Many earlier civilizations saw dreams as predictors of the future, or as signs and signals from the gods or spirits. By contrast, Freud and other psychoanalysts saw dreams as more egocentric and more personal, as indicators of what was really driving us as well as signals from the deepest crevices of our unconscious. These signals aren't easy to decode, according to Freud, because dreams are never what they seem—nothing as simple as snakes being a phallic symbol, or church steeples reflecting a need for spirituality. No, dreams are supposed to have deep, symbolic meaning, meaning that requires training to discern, because you yourself refuse to see the connections in them, and you hide their meaning under deep metaphoric layers. Still, according to Freud, analyzing them is worth it, because once we tease out those layers, we'll find echoes of the deep, buried trauma of our past that is actually causing our current problems, those traumas we talked about above that happened when you were too small and innocent to be blamed. Once you recognize the reality of those traumas, you can embrace them and bring them to consciousness, and then you'll know the real source of your problems, realize the buried trauma you've bee denying, and that insight will make you capable of recovering.

But wait, I hear the most skeptical among you say (no, my long distance hearing hasn't faded yet, even though according to my wife I seldom hear her even when she's standing next to me). If we can't remember our fears and traumas from the past because we've repressed them, how do we know they happened at all? Freud had two answers for that objection. The first one is more than a bit circular in nature. You must have had such a trauma, Freud would point out, because you're anxious and depressed, and anxiety and depression always comes from such childhood traumas, even if you don't remember them. Moreover, the very fact you don't remember them shows us how well-repressed they must be!

Freud's second answer was even more creative and involved than his first. You must have such buried traumas, because everyone experiences one of two universal traumas between the ages of 3 and 5. These two supposedly universal traumas were *castration* anxiety (obviously limited to boys), and *penis envy,* (an experience supposedly universal for girls). Thus, even if your parents didn't beat you or molest you, even if you were never abandoned, left to starve, or frightened with terrible tales, every one of you supposedly underwent a terrible trauma that has scarred you for life, a trauma you've repressed so strongly you don't remember it. This experience Freud named after a minor Greek ruler of antiquity, whose story was the subject of an Ancient Greek playwright's most famous work.

Oedipus Rex, literally, Oedipus the King, is a tragic and more than just a bit improbable tale based on an ancient Greek myth. It was penned by Sophocles and first performed in Greece somewhere around 429 B. C. E. (Sophocles, 1982). As a young prince visiting a neighboring king, Oedipus' father, Laius, commits an unforgivable indiscretion, resulting in his entire line of descendants being cursed. When Laius later becomes king and he and his bride, Queen Jocasta, consult the Oracle just after the birth of his son, Laius discovers that he is doomed to be killed by that newborn sometime in the future. King Laius orders Jocasta to kill their infant immediately and thus avoid his fate, but Jocasta hands the task over to an underling instead (infanticide apparently not being her cup of tea). That underling also can't bring himself to do the deed, so he abandons the baby in a field with his legs bound together (or perhaps staked to the ground—there are conflicting reports here). The baby is found by a shepherd who names him Oedipus, literally, "swollen feet." That shepherd passes the baby he has found on to another shepherd who takes him to a neighboring land, Corinth, where he is adopted by the local king and queen, Polybus and Merope, who happen to be conveniently childless (as well apparently being unbothered by infants of unknown providence who have swollen feet).

Everything then goes swimmingly for Oedipus for a time, until, as a young man, he hears a rumor that he is not actually Polybus and Merope's biological son. But when he asks the Oracle to name his true parents, the Oracle instead relates the undoubtedly highly disturbing news that Oedipus will kill his father and marry his mother. Despite the fact that he had gone to the Oracle precisely because he doubted that Polybus and Merope were his biological parents, Oedipus appears to forget that possibility, because he immediately assumes that the Oracle is saying he will kill Polybus and Merope. Being, apparently, a decent sort, he immediately flees to Thebes, hoping to spare the parents who raised him from the fate predicted by the oracle. (These characters in Greek dramas never seem to learn a fundamental point—you can't escape the fate decreed by the Oracle. In that respect they seem no smarter than modern day targets of the psychologically deranged in slasher movies.)

So of course, the Oracle will not be denied, and, in making Oedipus flee, it makes sure that he will fulfill his original destiny (It's rather a scheming, nasty little Ancient Wonder when you get right down to it). While trying to flee his fate, Oedipus immediately charges right into it. On the road at a particularly narrow spot, Oedipus meets Laius, his biological father, and in what may be the earliest documented case of road rage, Laius attacks Oedipus physically over whose chariot should have the right of way. Oedipus responds to being attacked by throwing Laius to the ground, where he strikes his head and inconveniently dies. Fleeing the scene of the murder, Oedipus next encounters the

Sphinx, who has been sent from her Ethiopian homeland to guard the gates of Thebes, allowing through only those who can answer her famous riddle, "What creature in the morning goes on four legs, at mid-day on two, and in the evening upon three?" Oedipus answers that the creature is man, who crawls on all fours as a baby, walks on two legs during the middle part of life, and then goes about on two legs and a cane in old age. The Sphinx, distraught at being bested, then throws herself off a cliff (either dramatic gestures were a part of the nature of sphinxes at the time, or she couldn't face having to come up with a new riddle.) Upon being told that her husband Laius has been killed, presumably by bandits, Queen Jocasta then offers her hand and the kingdom to Oedipus, apparently impressed by handsome young men who can make sphinxes off themselves. Naturally, in the nature of such stories, Oedipus has no clue that this veritable cougar of the Ancient World is his biological mother.

After some time, though, during which Oedipus, now Oedipus Rex, and the Queen have children of their own, a plague strikes Thebes, and Oedipus consults with his fortune teller to discover the cause of the plague. The fortune teller divines that the plague was due to the fact that King Laius' murderer had not been punished. Unaware that the man he killed on the road to Thebes was the king and thus he was the man in need of punishment, Oedipus then starts an investigation of Laius' murder. Ultimately, he unearths the fact that it was indeed he who killed Laius, and also that he was Laius' and the Queen's biological child. Despite all his efforts, he had killed his father and married his mother, just as the Oracle had decreed. Upon finding out that she was married to her son and the killer of her husband, Jocasta responds by hanging herself, and Oedipus, in despair over the many tragedies in his life, pokes his own eyes out with the long gold pins from her dress. The moral of the story appears to be that, ultimately, man cannot escape his destiny. (Or maybe the moral is that killing your father and marrying your mother, even inadvertently, is a bad idea. Then again, maybe we're supposed to conclude that improbable coincidence can even punk kings). That's not the end of the story, by the way. Oedipus lived on after blinding himself, at least long enough to appear in a sequel entitled *Oedipus at Colonus.* Like many sequels, though, this one also apparently failed to live up to the standards set by the original piece in either popularity or originality and is seldom remembered, let alone performed.

Enough about the very unlucky Oedipus and his very unlikely fate. Let's get back to Freud and his unlikely explanations instead. Freud was looking for some sort of trauma that all children must suffer that was so disturbing that they blocked out memories of early childhood, and he believed he'd found it in what he called the *Oedipus Complex.* Children, he reasoned, are totally dependent on their mothers, for care, for protection, and, most significantly in his mind, for breast feeding. (Freud rightly pointed out that we fathers don't tend to be very useful for that last task. Yet, is bottle feeding, a task fathers are just as equipped as mothers to do, really all that different, at least from the child's perspective? What did Freud think happened to infants who are bottle fed by their fathers, anyway?). As babies grow into toddlers and preschoolers, Freud argued, weaning just intensified children's needs to cling to their mothers in any way possible. In his mind, children fall in love with their mothers, and jealously want to possess them, just as Oedipus married and had children with his mother. Yet at this same time, mother appears to be pushing the child away, encouraging independence and demanding things of the child. No longer is the child welcome to crawl into mother's bed when he or she is frightened or lonely. Yet someone else is allowed to be close to mother, closer than the child who is being pushed away, and that person is Dad.

Yep, dear old Dad. He has mother, and he's not giving her up. Freud argued that the child sees the father as the impediment to his or her regaining his or her position with Mom, and jealously wants him to go away. But the child is smaller and much less powerful, and really has no way of displacing Dad, which just increases his or her jealousy further. Eventually, he or she wishes dear old Dad would just go away, or perhaps wishes he or she could terminate Dad with extreme prejudice.

And that, according to Freud, is about the time that the child makes a crucial connection. Sometime prior to this point, the child has probably noticed that there were people in the world whose bodies were different from their own. Toddler and preschool children of Freud's time were changed, dressed, bathed, and used the sanitary facilities openly around each other, very much as they do now. A child would have to be a complete moron not to notice that some people have equipment that other people lack. At this point, Freud thought that the pathways of boys and girls diverged. Boys, he thought, notice that some people lacked appendages that they themselves had . Girls, on the other hand, note that some people have appendages they themselves appear to lack. Neither sex may see much significance in those facts to start with. After all, people differ in lots of other ways, too. Most people have hair on their heads, but Grandpa Darrel doesn't. Uncle Jerry has a big white beard, but hardly anyone else does. Some people have short hair, some have curled hair, and some people's hair is straight and long. Some people have small noses, and some have giant honkers of prodigious dimensions. So people differ in all kinds of ways. Yet this particular difference matters more, according to Freud. Once preschoolers become incensed with jealousy over Dad's superior access to Mom's attention, this dichotomy of bodily construction acquires a deep significance. Boys develop what Freud called *castration anxiety,* and girls develop *penis envy.*

"Say what??!!" I hear you cry. Hey, don't blame me, I'm only the messenger. I'm no more responsible for this message than for Sophocles' Oedipus story line. Sigmund Freud believed that boys routinely decide that the "no penis people" must have had theirs

forcibly removed, probably by that powerful father that they themselves want to depose so badly.

A quick aside--Freud isn't using anything like proper terminology here. The word for removal of the penis would be *penectomy*. Castration, an operation often done on animals to reduce their aggressive tendencies and to make the meat of them more tender by preventing them from growing such tough muscles, involves the removal of only the testes, not the penis, and the operation generally leaves the penis itself intact and still functional. For that matter, Freud probably was referring to the belief that boys believed that penis, scrotum, and testes had all been removed from girls, a combination of both penectomy and castration. One wonders why, in naming this anxiety, Freud focused on what was to him the less significant testes rather than the more important penis. But perhaps I'm being anal by even mentioning this, and as I haven't discussed being anal yet (give me a few pages,) we'll let it go for now.

Getting back to the point (I always do eventually), Freud believed boys suffered traumatic fear of their fathers as a result of castration anxiety, a fear they dealt with eventually by burying it, forgetting their fearful memories, and instead trying to become as much like their fathers as possible so their fathers wouldn't see them as a threat. Then those boys supposedly moved on to looking for a girl just like the girl who married dear old Dad.

The process for girls was different, Freud believed. After all, you can't fear castration, or more properly, combination penectomy/castration, if it's supposedly already a done deal. Freud thought instead that girls suffer from *penis envy.* They see that boys have penises and they want one (because who wouldn't—they're just so darn cool—nothing like having a way to write your name in the snow with just a flick of the wrist). Then girls supposedly turn their attentions toward their fathers, who have the desired organ. But, as is the case with the boys, they're rebuffed by their powerful parents, in that Dad already has Mom, and Mom is metaphorically establishing a moving screen blocking the girl from Dad. So the girl instead turns her attention outward, trying to find a guy just like Dad so she can control his penis instead, and repressing the whole sordid attraction to her father while trying to act as much like her mother as possible. Freud thought that repressed trauma from the Oedipal complex caused sexual repression and other sexual problems in both boys and girls, and was responsible for sexual orientation as well.

How did Freud come to the conclusion that children go through these rather complex and convoluted traumas? You might assume that he interviewed and studied hundreds of children of preschool age as the basis for his conclusions, but you'd be wrong—Freud saw almost no children in therapy or otherwise—his client list consisted primarily of wealthy adult women. No, Freud developed his Oedipal ideas from two sources—analyzing his own childhood memories, and analyzing comments and admissions of his wealthy female patients.

Looking first at Freud's own childhood memories, let's examine what we know of Freud's parents. Sigmund Freud was the eldest son of what we'd now call a large family, although it wasn't all that large for his time. He had seven younger brothers and sisters (He also had two older step-siblings from his father's previous marriage, but they were not part of young Sigmund's household). His father was a wool merchant, a man who bought, sold, and traded wool. Wool was then and is now a commodity, and that means that prices fluctuated wildly and sometimes without rhyme or reason. This led to a bit of volatility in the Freud household—at times money could be quite tight, but other times the Freuds were quite well-off. Through good times and bad, though, the Freuds spared no expense in getting their brilliant oldest son the best education possible. That meant long work hours for Freud's father, who apparently was not deeply involved in the rearing of the children. He had strong expectations for his children, especially his oldest son, and set standards he expected the boy to live up to. But otherwise he was a rather emotionally-distant, reserved man focused on making a living. Freud's mother, on the other hand, was deeply involved in rearing her children and provided all of their emotional support. It wouldn't be terribly surprising that the oldest son in such a family would see his father as somewhat of a rival, a person who came home and usurped the attention young Sigmund's mother normally focused on her little prodigy.

Then we have Freud's patients. Freud began his practice in the 1880's and was world famous by the 1920's. Only wealthy women could afford extensive treatment for psychological problems at the time—the poor went largely untreated unless their problems were especially interesting. This was especially true of the patients of the famous Dr. Freud, because he charged three times the going rate for therapy once he became famous. On the balance, then, Freud's patients tended to be wealthy women. Being female, despite their wealth they were also surprisingly powerless. Wealthy girls in Austria at that time were pretty much the possessions of their fathers until they married, after which they become totally dependent upon their husbands. They had little choice in who they married or when—marriages were often arranged to cement family ties or further business empires. Women of society, as these wealthy women were, were strongly constrained concerning where they could go and what they could do—they had to maintain appearances, after all. They could not be involved in finances or business, and they had no say in major decisions in their lives. During the turmoil of WW I, and the financial chaos that followed that war and then the world-wide Great Depression, these women often could do nothing about the stresses and worries raised by their unstable society.

Under these circumstances, it isn't at all surprising that many of Freud's patients reported to him that they envied their brothers, or wish that they had been born male. Their brothers had some freedom in picking their wives, they participated in business and made family decisions, and they decided when the family would have children and how many they would have. These women's male counterparts got to pursue interesting careers, got to inherit the family business and family fortunes, and in general had much more to do than to stand on a figurative pedestal looking attractive. But when Freud's female patients voiced their feelings about their unfair positions in life, Freud took their wistful references to envying their brothers as support for his posited penis envy, rather than as an honest resentment of women's place in their society. So Freud argued that everyone, boys and girls, suffered such psychic trauma in the preschool years that they repressed the memories, thus suffering from what is known as *infantile amnesia.* In addition, he argued that traumas other than castration anxiety and penis envy also were routinely repressed in the years that followed—in fact, any upsetting memory of childhood, Freud argued, was repressed as a matter of course, thus protecting us from our anxieties.

But there was more to Freud's theory than Oedipal Complexes, castration anxiety, and penis envy. Freud was thoroughly versed in biology, and thus he was aware of the Theory of Evolution and its perspective that we must view human heredity in terms of what qualities promote the survival of our genes. Thus, he believed we all had basic biological drives of a genetic nature, and that like all animals these drives propel us through life. Freud referred to these basic drives of survival as the *id* (Literally, in German, "it.") The fact that the id drives us, though, doesn't mean we let the id control everything, according to Freud. We don't always eat even when we're very hungry, or drink when we're dying of thirst, or dive into sexual relations with everyone we find attractive. (Well, most of us don't, anyway.) No, we can control the id, using our own ability to reason and think rationally. This ability to reason and think rationally, Freud referred to as the *ego* (From the Latin word for "I" or "me"). The ego is our rational thought, which can control the id and channel it into the most acceptable paths toward satisfaction. (So, literally, "I" am controlling "it." My bodily drives are an "it," an animal thing not deserving of identity, whereas rational thought is the essence of "I" or "me." The id is animal, in Freud's view, the ego, human.)

Suppose, for example, that you're sitting in a conference room at work waiting for a meeting to start. You're hungry because you stayed up late watching "Dr. Who," (it was the Caves of Androzani episode—you couldn't miss that) and had to skip breakfast to make it to the meeting on time. A colleague plunks down beside you and sets down a paper plate holding the most beautiful glazed donut you've ever seen—a glistening sugar-encrusted culinary work of art. Your colleague then leaves the room, leaving the tempting toroid momentarily unguarded. Your id immediately begins making its needs known. "I want that," it says. "I'm hungry. Take that and eat it! It'll taste good!"

But you don't reach for the donut, because the ego then starts reasoning with the id. "You don't want that," it says, probably in a fussy, lecturing, superior tone of voice. "Donuts are full of transfats and loaded with calories. Besides, it's not even your donut, and if you eat someone else's donut there will be nasty consequences. So hold your horses, id, and when the meeting ends, we'll go get you a nice healthy rice cake to eat." (You've probably guessed by now the ego, which is driven by what Freud called "the reality principle," tends to interfere with our good times.) Your id may drive you to do things, but it's the ego that channels, controls, and steers that drive to acceptable ways of satisfying that id.

You can say "no" to donuts, and picking your nose in public, and eating your food at the restaurant until other people are served, primarily because you're an adult, with a fully developed, powerful ego. As you might suspect, Freud argued that toddlers are all id—impulsively trying to satisfy biological needs as soon as they come up without any care about the consequences. The ego develops as the child grows, in part because of parental insistence that the child restrain his or her biological urges. The two of them, id and ego, are constantly wrangling throughout our lives, in

Freud's view. Sometimes the id may overcome the ego and we'll do something ill-advised and impulsive (but oh, so satisfying!). Other times, Freud thought, the ego might control the person too tightly, not allowing the id's needs to be expressed and satisfied, and that could be problematic as well.

Freud introduced the id and the ego early on in his writings. Only after the passage of some time did it dawn on him that his theory needed a third personality component to complement the id and the ego. What drove him to this third component is the existence of emotions like guilt and pride. Freud recognized that we feel guilt when the ego fails to properly control and channel the id, and we feel pride when it does a particularly good job. Yet because those feelings deal with how well the id and the ego are working together (or fighting with each other tooth and nail, with figurative clumps of ego hair and bits of id flesh flying willy-nilly) they cannot originate from either personality component, but must instead be a product of a third component, a component that observes the id's and ego's interactions and judges them. This new component Freud called the *superego.* Freud's superego was very much like what we call our conscience—that little Jiminy Cricket we all carry around inside us. He believed that the superego developed in early childhood shortly after the appearance of the ego. Parental judgments of how well our egos are controlling our ids in these early years become voices inside our heads as we mature—voices that tell us how our parents would feel about our behavior were they present. So, once again, mothers and fathers are credited with having a great deal to do with how children turn out, by creating the child's superego, or failing to create it.

Continuing our short course on Freudian theory and terminology, Freud argued that the libido changed in its focus as children grew older, in that the sources of biological drives shifted. Newborns were said to be in the *oral stage.* Noting the desire of newborns and babies to suck on things, and the necessary role such sucking plays in the infant's survival, Freud posited that libido satisfaction centered on the mouth initially, and on obtaining relief from the powerful and basic drives of hunger and thirst through that orifice. If parents are relatively responsive during these helpless months of the child's life, Freud considered the oral need satisfied, and argued that the baby developed a basic sense of trust in the world. But if caretakers were lax, and the baby went hungry and thirsty for hours at times, or was fed more briefly than his or her greedy little personality desired, Freud argued that the lack of satisfaction of the oral drives created an oral personality, a personality marked by a lack of trust in others, and general pessimism and hostility.

Now here's where things get almost surreal again in Freudian theory. Because Freud argued that the oral stage of the first couple of years of life was followed by a demand by parents that the child start putting off some of the basic drives in order to fit more fully into the needs of the world. This demand for control over the libido's desires begins, Freud thought, with the onset of potty training, which is why this stage obtained the charming name of the *anal stage*. (An important aside here: potty training was often started prior to the child's first birthday in Freud's day. As you might expect from such an early start, though, parents were not immediately successful and experienced quite a battle with their children over this issue, a battle Freud blamed on willfulness on the part of the child rather than on the more likely total lack of conscious sphincter control at that age.)

In this anal stage, then, control of one's impulses becomes the major goal that parents have foisted upon the child, and, although this control may start with demands for potty training, it soon spreads to demands that the child sit still, not scratch in embarrassing places, not burp, not talk when others are talking, avoid running in the house, and a plethora of other restrictions that will haunt him or her for a lifetime. Freud argued that, if parents handle this stage right, the child will develop a sense of pride and self-satisfaction every time the ego successfully controls the id.

So what can go wrong at the anal stage? Push too hard, Freud thought, and the child may push back, developing pride in being able to resist parents and other people trying to control him or her rather than pride in controlling his or her own ego. The same thing may happen if you don't push the child hard enough—he or she may develop no sense of discipline and refuse to make the ego control the id. Alternatively, a parent who emphasizes control too much may end up with a child who is fanatic about control, developing the need to control every aspect of life. This latter group of people, who need to control everything, are who we're referring to when we call people *anal personalities*.

Note how, in typical Freudian style, everything that happens in the oral and anal stages is ultimately traceable back to parents. You don't trust others? It was your mother's fault for not caring for you assiduously enough. You're an incredible control freak—well, thank your mom for focusing too much on every little mistake and every little lapse. Nothing is your fault, and the present isn't that important—only your past treatment by others matters in the Freudian world.

Continuing on in the Freud universe, what happens next? After the child either takes pride in reasonable self control, becomes a fanatic about it, or rebels and refuses to be controlled, the preschooler enters the *phallic stage*. We've already talked quite a bit about the phallic stage, because this is the stage where the Oedipal conflict supposedly takes place, along with its concomitant trauma driven by castration anxiety or penis envy. If the child makes it successfully through these troubled waters, he or she identifies with the same sex parent and becomes fixated on and attracted to opposite sex partners. If not, the child could end up dealing with the whole sordid episode by denying their sexual feelings entirely and becoming powerfully sexually repressed, or could end up going completely the other way, becoming so fixated on attracting the parents and substitutes for the parents that he or she becomes promiscuous and vain. According to Freud, failure to resolve the Oedipal conflict could result in inappropriate sex role identification. Freud also thought that, at this stage, having an unusually strong, controlling mother and a weak, wimpy father could lead to homosexuality in both sexes. As we'll discuss in *Chapter 5: Male and Female, Vive la Difference!*, this Freudian view of the origins of transsexuality and of sexual orientation has been largely discredited.

Freud thought that the whole Oedipal complex was so frightening to most children that once it was resolved, all sex drive was repressed by children, and the energies of that drive were shunted into safer, more acceptable activities. Shifting the energies caused by one thing into something more socially acceptable is a process Freud labeled "sublimation." In this case, Freud argued that these sexual energies were shunted into mastery or accomplishment. Freud called this stage the *latency stage,* because he believed that sexual energies were not visible, but were nonetheless there, under the surface. He believed the latency period lasts from early childhood until adolescence, when sex drive finally bursts out again.

So does that complete suppression of sex drive really happen? There appears to be no question that children focus more and more on achievement and accomplishing things in the childhood years. But does that mean that all sexual drives had disappeared? Well, ask yourself that question. Did you lose all interest in sexual things at 5 and regain them again at puberty? If you're like most of us, probably not. My guess is that you maintained a low but significant interest in sexual issues and sexual activities throughout your childhood, possibly even including occasional sexual experimentation with other children as well as significant amounts of self-stimulation. I'm also betting that, if you're like most other children, you endeavored to keep this sexual interest and any sexual activity you engaged in under wraps, because you knew that the adults around you didn't approve of such things, and your peers were likely to mock you mercilessly if they discovered your secret.

Such sexual behaviors and interests by children were even more disapproved of in Freud's time, especially among females, the group that made up the bulk of his adult patients. This was a time when masturbation was considered a depraved habit that caused blindness, loss of strength, and a general wasting away, and a time that people believed that the loss of an ounce of semen was equivalent to the loss of a pint of blood. In Austria in Freud's time, children could be severely beaten if caught engaged in sexual experimentation, and girls who masturbated might be subjected to clitorectomy. So in Freud's time, even more than now, children's sexual feelings and activities went underground once they got old enough to recognize societal disapproval of such feelings and activities. (If you've read the previous book of this series, *Psychology in Plain English,* you'll recall from chapter 3 of that volume that punishment of children for a behavior often results in the behavior being hidden rather than stopping). Freud then interpreted this disappearance of visible sexuality as a sign of the disappearance of sexuality itself.

Freud's final psychosexual stage is the genital stage, the stage where we can satisfy our libidos in behaviors that are aimed towards attracting and keeping a partner and engaging in activities that might possibly result in producing offspring and thus enabling the perpetuation of our genes. Coinciding with the soaring hormone levels of puberty, this is the stage where sexual interests are supposed to burst out again, dominating our being and motivating us toward accumulating such things as money and power and focus on our appearances, all of which are things that make it possible for us to attract and keep sexual partners.

Freud thought that many adult problems arose because of problems in the psychosexual stages. A person could become *fixated* in a stage, for example, due to not resolving the big challenge of that stage. Such a person would then suffer psychopathology related to the fixation. A person fixated in the oral stage, for example, was said to be excessively focused on trust issues, often becoming pessimistic, overly needy, or passive and depressed. A person fixated in the anal stage would have control issues, being either a micromanager who had to have everything just so, or becoming excessively sloppy and messy to demonstrate that he or she couldn't be controlled. Problems in the phallic stage supposedly resulted in sex role identification problems, sexual identity problems, or homosexuality. Difficulties in the latency stage might lead to the person being excessively competitive or overly focused on material things and achievement.

More significantly, Freud also argued that most of these motivations for pathology were unconscious. Thus, people's mental problems were driven by unconscious conflicts, desires, and problems from deep in their childhoods. Not being aware of the actual causes of their problems, then, Freud believed that they mistakenly attributed their problems to other targets. He also argued that it isn't possible to solve such mental problems until the person makes the unconscious causes or motivations of his problems conscious. This is believed to be a lengthy and difficult process, possibly requiring many months or years of therapy, but a necessary one.

It never ceases to fascinate me that this belief of Freud's has permeated the consciousness of the public as much as it has. Many people, maybe a majority, believe that we all have buried unconscious conflicts stemming from childhood, that we routinely bury traumatic events rather than think about them, and that the only way to deal with such buried memories is to engage in psychodynamic therapy. Under the guidance of your analyst, you then have to dig deeply until you force the memories to the surface, where you can wallow in them and accept the experiences you've hidden as the cause of your problems.

By contrast, the new kid on the block in the therapy game, cognitive therapy, takes almost exactly the opposite tack in treatment. Cognitive therapists argue that you're anxious or depressed because you're dwelling on anxiety-causing or depression-causing thoughts, and the way to recover is to stop focusing on those things. Let's say your mother beat you when you were four. A Freudian therapist would encourage you to remember all the aspects of the trauma that you could, put yourself back into that place, try to remember how it made you feel, and perhaps even tell your mother what you should have told her back then, with the therapist standing in as a proxy to the mother if necessary. A cognitive therapist, on the other hand, would suggest that you stop thinking about the pains and wrongs and traumas of the past, and instead focus on what was and is positive and good about your life now. "You're not four," the cognitive therapist would say. "~~You're~~ Your mother's not beating you anymore. So what's your problem now?"

That's a pretty strong contrast. I mean, we've got two very influential traditions in psychology telling us to do two contradictory things. Which one should we follow? You might start by asking which one will make us feel better. That's a tougher thing to determine than it might at first appear. How do you define "better" in psychological terms? There's really no one standard—in fact, "better" is defined differently by different traditions of therapy. For psychodynamacists like Freud, the patient is better if the unconscious memories and conflicts have been unearthed and are now conscious. But for cognitive therapists, the patient is better if he or she is happier and less bothered than in the past. Often, this would involve not unearthing memories that bother you, but rather *burying them more deeply*!

And it gets more complicated than that when you look even closer. The goal of improvement for psychodynamics may sound clearly defined—when you've become consciously aware of your unconscious conflicts and memories and dealt with them, you'll get better. But how do we know for sure when we've become consciously aware of our unconscious conflicts and memories? How do we know that the memory we've just unearthed is the one causing the problem, or the conflict we've just become aware we have is the conflict that's really bothering us? Perhaps this isn't the real memory or conflict after all—perhaps there's some other, more deeply unconscious conflict that's the real problem, a conflict that we're avoiding and hiding by focusing on the current one we've just unearthed. How do we know that you won't be back next year, with new symptoms that have occurred because you haven't dealt with the real conflict yet? For that matter, how do we even know that the conflict that you've just "unearthed" was actually ever there to start with, rather than just being manufactured obligingly by the patient because the therapist keeps insisting that it ought to be there?

Wait, it gets even more nebulous. Let's go back to dream analysis. Freud thought his dream analysis theory was his very best work, the thing for which he'd be known. He even published lengthy volumes describing various dream contents and noting how to interpret the unconscious meanings or symbols of these contents.

For example, dreaming of moving water, such as roaring rivers, supposedly signaled an unconscious desire for, or fear of, change. Dreaming of having a tooth extracted was symbolic of an unresolved castration anxiety.

Let me give you an example of psychodynamic dream analysis as reported by Seligman, Walker, and Rosenhan in their textbook, *Abnormal Psychology* (2001). It involves a patient by the name of Ann, who was in love with two different men simultaneously, or so she reported. After deliberating for 6 months, she finally made the decision to marry Michael. That night, she had a dream that she reported to her psychologist the next day. In it, it was nighttime, dark, and raining. She was climbing a fire escape with a big box protected under her raincoat. Sneaking into her room, she carefully double-locked the door, then opened the box, which she now realized was a treasure chest. Inside were rubies and emeralds and diamonds.

The therapist argued that the symbolic meaning of this dream hinged on her unconscious association of the name of her rejected suitor, Jules, with the jewels that were the contents of the box. It was an easy jump from there to the conclusion that she still secretly wanted and desired Jules despite her decision to marry Michael (hiding the box under her coat, sneaking up the fire escape, and double-locking the doors being all signs of her desire for secrecy about her attraction to him).

Yet is that the only possible interpretation of the dream? Chances are if we knew a bit more about the two men, we could probably find just as many cues in the dream suggesting a satisfaction with the decision to marry Michael. We might find that Michael is wealthier than Jules, for example, and we could interpret the dream as Ann choosing wealth, as represented by diamonds and emeralds and rubies. Or we might find that Michael has emerald green eyes, or that he's a jeweler. The number of other possible interpretations of the dream are endless.

That's the problem—humans are really, really good at making connections between things. In fact, we're so good at it, that we can even make connections where there were no connections originally. One consequence of this ability is our incredible ability to create conspiracy theories. For example, right after the attacks on the World Trade Center in New York in 2001, an email conspiracy claim circulated everywhere claiming that Microsoft, Jews, or both were somehow complicit in the attacks, and that this complicity goes back many years. As evidence, this conspiracy claim suggested typing in the phrase Q33 NY, supposedly the number of one of the flights that crashed into the towers, then highlighting that phrase and changing it into the "Wingdings" font. When you do, you get ✈▤▤ ☠✡, a juxtaposition that is rather disturbing at first consideration. The average person, seeing deep meaning in such a symbolic grouping, tends to immediately assume that if they can interpret the symbols a particular way, that must be their meaning. Someone in the fonts creation department of Microsoft must have known about the planned attacks years beforehand—someone either with a connection to Jews or wishing death to Jews!

Here's the problem with that conclusion. First off, the little boxes in Wingdings font are actually supposed to represent printed pages, not buildings. The fact that we can interpret them as looking like buildings doesn't mean that's what they symbolized to start with. Second, the final two symbols have multiple possible interpretations when juxtaposed—they could mean "death to Jews," "death by Jews," "danger to Jews," "a warning to Jews," or, for that matter, a warning not to drink Mogen David wine. Third, and most significant, the phrase Q33 NY has no direct connection to the World Trade Center attacks whatsoever. It isn't the number of any of the flights involved in the attacks nor the tail number of the aircraft on those flights. American Airlines Flight 11 bore tail number N334AA, American Airlines Flight 77 bore tail number N644AA, United Airlines Flight 93 bore tail number N591UA, and United Airlines Flight 175 bore tail number N612UA. Indeed, the letter/number combination Q33, supposedly the flight number of one of the aircraft, appears to have been chosen simply because they create an intriguing and meaningful picture when converted to the Wingdings font.

What happens if we convert one of the real tail numbers to the Wingdings font? Fascinating things, really. Let's look at one of them that I picked at random.

N644AA =☠⌛🗐🗐✌✌

The first symbol is the skull and crossbones, which might be "danger," or "death." The second is supposed to be an hourglass, but it could be interpreted as a man in a robe and turban if you've got a good imagination. The next two symbols are supposed to be stacks of documents in Wingdings, but they could be seen as three dimensional tower representations, or as a representation of towers starting to collapse. And the last two symbols might be interpreted as "victory," or "peace," or as "rabbits in sunglasses," for that matter. Put it together and we have a man in a turban bringing death and destruction to the twin towers and celebrating victory twice, once for each tower. Pretty scary, huh?
But wait, before we get hasty, let's type something else in and convert it to Wingdings. How would you interpret this next set of pictorials?

✋ ☹⚐✞☜ ✡⚐✞

Looks pretty ominous to me. I see a hand cautioning us to wait.

Then there seems to be a very unhappy face, symbolizing mourning or sadness, followed by a waving banner, perhaps a symbol of a marching army or a call to war. Then you have the finger pointing at a cross, clearly a sign that the mourning or sadness is due to a war on Christianity (or perhaps a war started by Christians). And who is that war between? The final sequence spells it all out—it's a war between Judaism and Christianity, right?

You could interpret it that way. Or perhaps the final grouping suggests Christianity and Judaism will unite together to fight the foe. Or perhaps we should view this set of symbols one of the myriad other ways you could interpret them. So what nasty, ominous phrase, when converted to the Wingdings font resulted in this disturbing message? The phase, "I love you."

The point, besides the fact that conspiracy theories are usually pointless wastes of your valuable time, time you could spend reading books like this one, is that humans are so good at interpretation and at tying things to other things that we can usually do it even when there's no actual tie there. So when it comes to dream interpretation, as they say in *Apollo 13,* "Houston, we have a problem." Sure, we can interpret practically every dream. But how do we ever know if we got the correct interpretation? How do we know that the dream actually meant anything to start with, other than random memories and thoughts that happened to come up while we're in REM sleep?

The short answer is that we can't ever know if we've got the "right" interpretation of the dream, and neither can your therapist. Even if you can interpret a dream to mean something, we have no way of knowing if that meaning was actually in the dream. Did Ann really secretly desire Jules, or did her dream mean something else, or nothing at all? We'll never know.

So are our problems really the result of unconscious, deeply buried conflicts and childhood traumas? Many people believe so. They often cite as evidence the fact that some people get better when they undergo psychodynamic therapy. But the causal factors in the improvement of people undergoing therapy aren't at all clear. It's possible that just by pointing the finger at a particular factor and saying, "That's why I was depressed," or "That's why I was upset" is sufficient to convince us that things will be better in the future, and thus that we should dig in and go on with life. Albert Bandura, famous social learning theorist, has argued that all therapies succeed to the degree that they change people's sense of self-efficacy, or their belief that they can do things. Bandura argues that it doesn't even matter what therapy or other influence causes the improvement in the sense of self-efficacy, only that the sense of self-efficacy improves. If you can convince yourself you've found the cause of your problems and that this cause can be changed, you'll probably face the future in a more optimistic state.

So we don't necessarily have to dig out our repressed memories and acknowledge them in order to get better. In fact, despite the fact that repressed memories are among the unconscious influences that are the linchpin of Freudian therapy, it's not actually clear that we repress even traumatic memories, let alone that we do so routinely. Pope, et. al reviewed 77 studies involving more than 11,000 child and adult victims of traumas. These people's experiences ranged from being an eyewitness to the Holocaust and living through it to seeing people they loved maimed and killed in explosions, being kidnapped, witnessing sexual assaults of their mothers, almost dying in floods and losing their families to them, living through fatal plane crashes, and being victims of rape. Only those who were extremely young at the time (under age 5) had any difficulty remembering the incidents they had witnessed and been part of. Everyone else in those 77 studies remembered the events in question, most of them remembering the events vividly and in great detail. Clearly, children and adults over the age of 5 routinely remember even very traumatic experiences, and there appears no general tendency to repress such memories. Yet, if one was going to repress memories, wouldn't these be exactly the ones that would be repressed?

What about reports of people who claim to have repressed memories and then recovered them through memory recovery therapy? Although such experiences are a mainstay of many books and movies and TV shows, corroboration of the truth of such reports is largely lacking in the scientific literature. In a survey of many such reports, Brandon, et. al, concluded in their 1998 article that, "No evidence exists for the repression and recovery of verified, severely traumatic events, and their role in symptom formation has yet to be proved... Given the prevalence of childhood sexual abuse, even if only a small proportion are repressed and only some of them are subsequently recovered, there should be a significant number of corroborated cases." They noted in their article that most reports of repressed memories being recovered involve events for which there is no way to verify truth of the "memory," and that the phrase "repressed memory" is often mistakenly used to describe memories that the person was fully aware of, and thus wasn't repressing at all. Yet if events that momentous don't trigger memory repression, is it likely that you repress your more mundane anxieties and worries?

Freud's Contributions

The bottom line is that, although American culture has swallowed Freudian theory whole and integrated it into movies, television, and popular lore, large parts of the theory itself are impossible to verify empirically or are more or less refuted by experimental data. That doesn't mean that Freud's contributions to psychology are negligible, however. Some of Freud's best work is the work he himself considered the most unimportant.

Let's start with Freud's popularization of the idea of unconscious processes. It may not be true that all our problems stem from them, but there's no question that we're sometimes driven by unconscious thoughts and desires. That doesn't necessarily mean that such thoughts and motives are repressed because, as Freud believed, they are too painful to deal with. It may just mean that we run on autopilot a lot of the time, following patterns we learned long ago, so long ago we've forgotten, consciously, why we react as we do. For example, constantly being teased by your two older brothers whenever you make a statement may create a classically-conditioned alarm reaction whenever anyone criticizes you at all, a reaction that means you're hypersensitive now. You could have that unconscious reaction even if you don't consciously remember being made fun of now. (Not that I'm talking about any particular little brother with two older brothers here. Really. Honestly! It's just an example! I swear! Why do you constantly have to attack me!)

What else did Freud himself undervalue in his theory? Ask many modern-day psychologists and they'll argue that Freud's best work is his set of defense mechanisms. These are mechanisms for dealing with worry or anxiety. Freud proposed a number of such mechanisms, varying in their maturity and their efficacy. For example, among the most primitive of defense mechanisms, according to Freud, was *repression.* Repression is the defense mechanism Scarlett O'Hara uses to great effect multiple times in *Gone with the Wind.* Every time she faces a crisis that seems too much to bear, including Rhett's final, memorable departure, Scarlett tosses her head and says, "I won't think about that now, I'll think about that tomorrow." The she proceeds to focus her attention somewhere else, while simultaneously working very hard not to think about the absent Mr. Butler.

A more advanced defense mechanism, according to Freud, is *projection.* Projection involves seeing the disturbing behavior or the anxiety that is troubling us in other people, so that they become the problem and not us. Walk into any neighborhood bar, sit down on a stool, and start talking quietly with one of the regulars at the bar, and it's likely that sooner or later he'll confide that, although he's got his drinking under control, the rest of his buddies have a fairly serious drinking problem. Then you can move to the other end of the bar, and odds are the person there will tell you the same thing. "I can take or leave the stuff," he'll say. "But the rest of these guys have a problem."

Intellectualization or *rationalization* is a bit more advanced, also. It involves dealing with the anxiety-causing or disturbing situation by coming up with rational excuses or reasons for the behavior, reasons that have nothing to do with the real reasons the person is doing the thing, but are much less anxiety-provoking and reflect better upon the individual. The finest rationalization of my generation, I've always believed, was this one: "Playboy? I only read it for the articles."

The Freudian defense mechanism that causes the most controversy, though, is undoubtedly *reaction formation.* In reaction formation the person deals with his or her anxiety or disturbance by visibly adopting actions and expressing attitudes that are exactly the opposite of what he or she really feels. Then the person can deny those feelings entirely, using these visible actions as evidence. Thus, the person using reaction formation would probably become extremely passionate in opposing the very thing he or she favored, or favoring the very thing he or she opposes. Freud didn't make a lot of friends with this one. After all, he's suggesting that, if you seem unusually fervent in opposing or championing a particular issue or cause, perhaps it's because, secretly, you feel the opposite. Trying to stamp out prostitution? Freud might suggest you're secretly fascinated by it. But by virulently opposing it, you can convince others, and even yourself, that you're one of the good guys, yet at the same time you can immerse yourself in prostitution, talk about it, and revel in the actions of the players in that world.

Take, for example, the very powerful homophobic attitudes of some males. Adams, et. al (1996) investigated the possibility that such attitudes could be due, at least in part, to such people having a secret attraction to other males and dealing with that attraction through reaction formation, by displaying anti-homosexual attitudes (and perhaps even convincing themselves that this hostility reflected their true feelings). They included 44 undergraduates in their study, all of whom professed to be heterosexual people. They gave this group a questionnaire measuring their levels of homophobia. After that, the men were shown videotapes depicting explicit heterosexual, male homosexual, and female homosexual activity, while hooked to a penile plethysmograph, a fiendish little device that precisely measures degree of male arousal. Homophobic men showed arousal to the male homosexual videos, but the non-homophobic men showed no such arousal. Adams and company concluded that at least some homophobic males may actually be attracted to homosexual activity, although it was not clear if they were aware of the attraction and were denying it, or whether they were unaware of the attraction and it was influencing them in some sort of unconscious, Freudian fashion. Either way, this would be classic Freudian reaction formation.

The most sophisticated and ultimately mature defense mechanisms, according to Freud, are *sublimation* and the use of humor. Freud thought both of these released the energies created by our anxieties, allowing them to be used for other purposes. Sublimation involves accepting that we do have the anxiety or disturbing thought, and taking the energy it creates and devoting it to positive activities. Consider, for example, a person who is fascinated by blood and gore. If he were to use repression, he'd try not to think about his fascination. Projection, on the other hand, could involve him convincing himself that the rest of his peers are unhealthily fascinated by blood and gore to an extent much worse than him. Rationalization might involve him arguing that he was fascinated not by the blood and gore, but by the construction of the body and the way systems are damaged when accidents occur. If a person fascinated by blood and gore were to use reaction formation, he might start a campaign to ban bloody scenes in movies and on TV. But a person using sublimation might accept that he's fascinated by blood and gore, and try to do something positive with it, perhaps becoming a surgeon, or a prop-creator for slasher films (films where people discover they're being stalked and then immediately split up).

So where does Freud stand today? It's hard for any theory in any social science to last for an extended period of time. The problem is that theorists retire and then die, whereas the scientific community continues to churn out new data at prodigious rates. While a theorist is still working in the field, he or she can examine that new data and then alter the theory to explain it. If Freud were alive today, he'd not only be incredibly old (over 150 at this point) but he'd have continued to evolve his theory to adjust to new data. Once a theorist retires (and especially once that theorist passes away), the theory gets frozen in whatever state it was when last revised by the theorist. As a lot of data has been published since Freud's time, quite a bit of it poses problems for his original theory. In addition, the best parts of Freud's theory have been incorporated into other theories and become part of mainstream psychology. This includes his idea of the unconscious mind and of unconscious influences, his defense mechanisms, his recognition that childhood experiences can influence adult thinking and behavior, and his recognition, radical at the time, that children can have sexual feelings and thoughts. That body of work alone is enough that Freud should be honored in the history of psychology, even if some of his more flamboyant and some of his more popular ideas haven't been so strongly supported.

Still, I'm looking forward to the day when "penis envy" merely means someone is hogging all the goober peas.

References:

Adams, H. E., Wright, L. W., Jr., & Lohr, B. A. (1996). Is homophobia associated with homosexual arousal? *Journal of Abnormal Psychology, 105*, 440–445.

Bandura, A. (1977). Self-efficacy: Toward a unifying theory of behavioral change. *Psychological Review*, *84,* 191-215.

Brandon, S., Boakes, D., Glaser, S., and Green, R. (1998). Recovered memories of childhood sexual abuse. Implications for clinical practices. *British Journal of Psychiatry*, *173*, 296-307.

Pope, H.G., Oliva, P.S. & Hudson, J. I. (2002). Scientific Status of Research on Repressed Memories. In D.L. Faigman, D.H.Kaye, M.J. Saks & J. Sanders (Eds.) Modern Scientific Evidence. St. Paul: West Group.

Seligman, M. E. P., Walker, E. F., & Rosenhan, D. L. (2001) *Abnormal Psychology(4th Edition).* New York: Norton.

Sophocles. (1982). *The three theban plays*. Robert Fagles, translator, Bernard Knox, Ed. New York: Penguin.

Chapter 2: A Bird in the Hand, or, You Don't Know What You've Got 'til it's Gone

When a dog bites a man, that is not news, because it happens so often. But if a man bites a dog, that is news. Quote usually attributed to New York Sun journalist John B. Bogart, but possibly originating with British newspaper publisher Alfred Harmsworth.

Don't it always seem to go
That you don't know what you've got 'til it's gone?
They paved paradise
And put up a parking lot.
Joni Mitchell, *Big Yellow Taxi*

The Availability Heuristic

Humans are the original organic computers. We pattern match better than any machine ever made, to the point where people can recognize old friends 20 years later even though hair loss, wrinkles, and all the other inexorable consequences of aging that I know so well have taken their toll. Yet, although we can pattern match like crazy, we also have a big, big limitation in our computing abilities. We can only think about small numbers of things at one time. If we try to think about more things, then other things that we were thinking about are typically lost in the process. We've worked out ways of dealing with this over the years, ways of limiting how many things we have to keep in memory simultaneously. We developed written languages, and then media for storing written language, running the gamut from clay tablets, through paper, magnetic tape, floppy disks, hard drives, and the Internet cloud. All of these supplement our memories, and make material available again when we need it. Still, all of these merely constitute supplements to our memories—we remain highly limited in how many things we can keep in mind at one time.

There is a serious consequence to this limitation. It makes it difficult to make decisions that involve a lot of data, because we can't keep all that information in our heads at the same time. So we take shortcuts. We come up with ways to narrow the number of things we have to keep in mind at once to manageable numbers. That means we don't exhaustively search for all examples of a particular situation when we're facing a task like judging how likely a particular event is—we merely retrieve a few examples and make our judgment from them.

For example, a friend of yours says he's going on a visit to Boca Raton, Florida (Nothing quite so fun as visiting a place whose name translates, literally, as "Mouse's Mouth.") If you truly care about him, you'll probably give some thought to whether he is going to face any danger by going there. (Actually, come to think of it, you'd probably give some thought to whether he faced any danger even if you despised him, but in that case you'd be rooting for the danger.) It would take considerable time and effort to research the experiences of all the people who've gone to beautiful Mouse's Mouth in order to determine just what dangers they've suffered and how serious those dangers were and what the rate of experiencing each of those dangers was. So we don't—we take a shortcut. The way that most of us usually make such judgments is to do a quick search of our own memories for readily retrievable examples of people who suffered exposure to danger or come to grief in Mouse's Mouth. If we can easily retrieve such memories, we judge that such dangerous incidents are frequent there. If we can't, we judge that he's apt to be safe, and wish him bon voyage.

This rule of thumb that we follow, where we tend to judge how likely an event is by how easily we can retrieve an example of it, is known as the *availability heuristic.* A heuristic is a problem-solving strategy that appears promising but doesn't guarantee a solution (as opposed to an algorithm, which is a problem-solving strategy that does guarantee a solution). The availability heuristic how easily we can retrieve memories of an incident or situation in order to judge how common the thing is or how likely it is to occur. Like most heuristics, the availability heuristic exists and is used because it often works for us. In general, we have more readily available memories of common occurrences, whereas we are far less likely to remember examples of less common situations.

But it doesn't always work this way, and for that, we can place the blame most specifically on the news media. Television, radio, Internet, and cable news organizations may be different media, but as a group the operators of all of them are motivated by the need to attract and keep listeners. That motivation, of necessity, affects what they report, and how they report it. Sensational, attention-getting stories with spectacular videos get lots of play, and so do very violent stories, very scary stories, emotion-gripping stories, and giant disasters. More significantly to our discussion, rare events get much more play on the news than common ones, simply because common events are not going to attract viewers. As in the Harmsworth quote at the beginning of this chapter, when a dog bites a man, that common occurrence is not going to make the news. But if a man were to bite a dog, that would be picked up by every news outlet, and the video would get a million hits on Youtube.

Which means that a lot of relatively rare events get considerable play from news outlets, and thus are likely to be part of our memories. For example, a few years back there was a brief period during which the news media became aware of the existence of *necrotizing fasciitis*. Necrotizing fasciitis is a rare bacteriological condition in which massive infection of a body part by a variety of different bacteria can lead to rapid deterioration and death of large areas of flesh, and for that reason is often referred to as the "flesh eating disease." The epithet "flesh eating disease" is a bit of a misnomer, in that the flesh isn't actually eaten by the bacteria but is instead killed by the bacteria's toxic waste products, but that's really not important to our discussion. What's important is two facts --necrotizing fasciitis, while horrific, is quite rare, and it isn't new, nor is it any more common than it's ever been. As far as rarity goes, there are perhaps a thousand new cases in the United States every year. That sounds like a lot, but when you consider that there are over 300 million Americans, that's an incidence of only 1 in 300,000 people. It's also been around for as far back as medical history goes.

Technically, therefore, the existence every year of a thousand new cases of necrotizing fasciitis is not news.. But reporters had never heard of it, apparently, so it was news to them, and they wrote all sorts of heart-tugging stories featuring people who were victims. Other people, seeing this sudden spate of stories, concluded that necrotizing fasciitis had suddenly burst forth and that they and their loved ones were in imminent danger of contracting the disease, merely because they could easily recall examples of people (from news reports) who had it.

Or consider the likelihood of being bitten by a shark. There are usually fewer than 50 shark attacks in a given year in the United States, and that includes all the coastal states, even Hawaii. (Florida generally accounts for more than half the total, although

I'm not sure what proportion occur in Boca Raton. Perhaps it should be called *Boca del Tiburon*, or *Shark's Mouth*). The number of people actually killed by sharks worldwide in a given year is usually just a handful, seldom more than 10. Yet after the movie *Jaws* came out in 1975, people's fears of the beach and of being killed by sharks skyrocketed. Few attacks actually occurred, but thanks to this popular movie, everyone could vividly bring up mental images of shark attacks occurring, and this ability to readily remember such attacks made us judge those attacks as being much more likely.

Sadly, this kind of misjudgment doesn't just cause unnecessary fear of relatively uncommon threats. It also affects public policy. People who, because of the availability heuristic, judge rare situations as being much more common, are also most likely to be willing to spend large amounts of public funds to combat such uncommon threats. "So what's the harm?" You ask. "We're just being cautious." But public money doesn't come from nowhere. it comes from the public coffers, coffers with only limited amounts of money in them to start with. Money spent on relatively rare threats isn't available to combat other threats, threats that may be much more likely to pose a real danger to us.

Here's an experiment you can try yourself—ask one of your adult friends whether he or she is more likely to be struck by lightning in a given year, or to die in a commercial jetliner crash. According to the National Weather service, (National Weather Service, 2010) your odds of being struck by lightning in a given year aren't even as great as your odds of contracting necrotizing fasciitis, only roughly 1 in 500,000. (That's the odds of being struck by lightning—lightning **deaths** are 10 times less common than that). But your odds of being killed by a commercial jetliner in the US in that same year is even lower than your odds of being struck by lightning—over the last 5 years, the number of airliner fatalities per year in the U. S. has averaged 138, or one in more than 2 million people. (Some years look even better for our airborne aluminum behemoths—in 2007, 2008, and 2010, there were no commercial aircraft fatalities at all in the United States). So you're quite a bit more likely to be struck by lightning than to die in a commercial jetliner crash, and neither thing people fear is particularly likely.

By comparison, an average of 36,676 people have died each year in car accidents in the United States over the last 5 years, or one in 7,700 people. You are almost 300 times more likely to die in a car accident than to die in a commercial jetliner. So tell me, why do people get into cars to go places without a thought about whether they'll be in danger during the ride or not, yet so many fear getting into commercial jetliners?

I've asked people this question, and gotten many answers. Some report that they feel in control in cars, but are at the mercy of the pilot in airplanes. But that can't be the primary reason—people who aren't driving, but merely riding with others, also step blithely into automobiles. And even if you **are** driving, you can't control the other drivers you're whizzing by with just inches separating you.

Others have argued that there are fewer airplanes overall, so that there are fewer airplane accidents for that reason. But even when expressed in terms of passenger miles, airliners have far fewer fatalities than cars. (So do commercial buses and passenger trains) (US Department of Transportation Pipeline and Hazardous Materials Safety Administration, 2010).

That leaves us back at the availability heuristic. Automobile accidents are so common they're seldom reported on TV news unless they're particularly horrendous or involve some starlet doing something such as running over the foot of a member of the paparazzi. Commercial jetliner crashes, in part because they're visually vivid and in part because they're exceedingly rare, get maximum coverage for days afterward, including extensive footage of wreckage, interviews of survivors, and computer-generated in-flight sequences of the final moments of the flight. As a result, pretty much all of us can recall vivid examples of numerous airplane accidents, but few can recall fatal car accidents, even though the latter are much more common. Through our reliance on the availability heuristic, this leads many to underestimate the risks of car accidents, and overestimate the risks of commercial airplane accidents.

In terms of public policy, this often means that we spend millions of dollars to deal with relatively unlikely threats to airline safety, while scrimping on spending for auto safety. For example, many airliners carry life vests and life rafts on board in case of the "unlikely event of a water landing." The odds that a commercial jetliner will ditch in a body of water in circumstances where the passengers survive and are saved by life vests and life rafts is so low as to be almost nil. The costs of carrying the weight of all those life-rafts and life vests around on flight after flight is considerable. A single 46-person life raft for a Boeing 747 weighs 100 pounds, for example, and it would take 8 such rafts to handle the passengers on such an airliner. Eight hundred pounds may not sound like much weight for a vehicle that can carry up to 200 tons, but that translates into room for three or four more passengers and their seats and baggage. Over the thousands of flights that 747 will make during its service life, that's quite a lot of money.

Actually, the savings of a few pounds is significant enough that All Nippon Airways not long ago experimented with a pilot program in which they politely asked passengers to visit the bathroom before flying, because they'd calculated that the overall weight reduction involved would save a significant amount of fuel and reduce the flight's carbon footprint as well as fuel costs. I know what you're saying—how much weight could that come to, half a pound a person? But on a 747-400 loaded with 500 passengers, half a pound a person adds up to 250 pounds, or enough to carry an additional passenger and his or her baggage. Over thousands of flights, that's a lot of money, too.

Requiring people to hit the head before flying, though, isn't currently required by law. But airlines are required to carry flotation devices when flying over water, even though such devices have saved few lives, and carrying them adds up to considerable cost with little in the way of return. Automobiles, on the other hand, often lack side door stiffeners and side airbags, even though it's far, far more likely they'll be needed, and they'll save considerably more lives. It's perceived risk, though, not actual risk that determines how we spend our money.

Another area where people tend to overestimate the likelihood of an event due to constant publicity involves marital infidelity. We hear of so many cases of infidelity in the tabloid news that many people think that the number of men and women who are unfaithful to their committed partners is quite large. Indeed, I've heard some folks (mostly women) who have proclaimed that most men are unfaithful, and women who don't agree are simply blind or in denial. So what are the odds that the average man or woman in the United States will be unfaithful to his or her partners?

Although data on fidelity are somewhat sensitive and difficult to obtain, it isn't impossible to obtain. All you really need to do is get a representative sample of Americans, convince them that their personal data will never be reported in such a way that it can be tied to them by anyone, and then allow them to divulge their own behavior in the strictest confidence. Edward Laumann and his colleagues did precisely that, concluding that fully 75% of married men and 85% of married women were faithful to their spouses (Laumann, 2001). The reaffirmed data from the past that suggests that Americans tend to be what we call "serial monogamists." Even people who've had many partners tend to stick with just one partner at a time, and infidelity is the exception, not the rule, despite what most people think. While it's possible that Laumann's data are flawed, it's more likely that it's simply our assessment of the likelihood of monogamy that's faulty, an assessment that's based on over-reliance on the availability heuristic.

Is a Bird in the Hand Worth a 50% Shot at Two in the Bush?

The fact that we can't trust our gut judgments of the likelihood of events is one of the reasons that we absolutely have to depend upon scientifically collected data and statistics to make reasoned judgments. In order to look at more evidence of this necessity, we will next consider the relative value of what one has compared to what one doesn't have. Is a bird in the hand really worth more than two in a bush?

Putting aside the issue of why you'd want a bird in your hand to start with, there's evidence that we value what we already have over comparable things that we don't currently have. Suppose, for example, that I give you a valuable, limited edition, exquisitely-crafted *Psychology in Plain English* commemorative coffee mug, with a retail value of $5.00. After letting you spend some time admiring it (a necessity—it's quite a handsome bit of crockery, really), I offer to let you keep the mug, or trade it for a lottery ticket that gives you a one out of ten chance of winning a larger, fancier *Psychology in Plain English* commemorative liquid refreshment vessel with a built in Blue-ray drive, valued at $50. Would you make the trade?

Statisticians analyze such deals in terms of what they call "expected value," or "expected utility." Expected utility is simply the sum total of the worth of the thing you're contemplating. So suppose you do have one of my extremely cool and rare $5 mugs (I really should up the price of those things, shouldn't I? I'm not even covering the manufacturing costs here.) The expected utility of this fine quality mug can be quantified fairly easily—it's $5, because that's what all the people clamoring to have one of their own have to part with to obtain one of these valuable items.

Now, what's the expected value of the deal I'm offering in trade? If you were to take the ticket that gives you a one out of ten chance of getting the commemorative liquid refreshment vessel with Blue-ray drive, worth $50, then that ticket also has an expected utility of $5. (Think of it this way—if you bought all ten tickets, thus assuring that you won this fabulous liquid refreshment vessel, the ten tickets would net you a mug worth $50, so each ticket must be worth $5.)

In terms of expected value, both the exquisitely-crafted $5 mug and one ticket for a one out of ten chance at the fabulous liquid refreshment vessel worth $50 are the same. So what if you had the mug, and I asked you if you wanted to trade for the chance to get the more fabulous version? You might expect that people would just as readily exchange the ticket for the mug as the mug for the ticket, because both have the same expected utility, and that they would be equally happy to get either the mug or the ticket. But as Daniel Kahneman and Amos Tversky discovered back in the 70's, that isn't what happens. When it comes to gaining something good (and the *Psychology in Plain English* mug is simply fabulous), people prefer the sure thing over the less sure, even when expected utility is the same. Most folks would take the certainty of having the less valuable mug over the far less sure chance of gaining a much more valuable one. They prefer small gains that are much more likely over larger potential gains that are less likely (Kahneman & Tversky, 1979).

Thus, if you already have a bird in your hand, and you have the choice of keeping it or letting it go for the 50% chance of catching two birds, most folks will keep the bird they have. The expected utility of the less probable gain has to be quite a bit greater before people will take a chance at giving up the sure thing for a less sure, more valuable thing. This creates a sort of trade inertia, in that most people have to see quite a bit of advantage before abandoning what they have for the chance at something better. Having odds of being just as well off in the new situation doesn't cut it—most people won't take on additional risk unless the odds are that they'll be substantially better off after the trade.

But what if the situation doesn't involve gains to you, but losses? What if, instead of giving the person a small sure prize or the chance for a more fabulous one, the person was faced with a possible cost? Suppose that Lutwidge parks in a loading zone and gets a $50 ticket. Then his friend tells him that, because of some data processing problems at City Hall, if he just ignores the ticket there's only a 10% chance that anyone will ever follow up on it and discover he didn't pay. On the other hand, if he is among the unlucky 10%, he'll then owe $500 in fines for failure to pay. The expected utility of paying right now is a loss of $50, and the expected utility of not paying right now is also a loss of $50, because out of every ten people who don't pay initially, nine pay nothing and the other one pays $500, averaging out to $50 apiece. The expected utility is the same for both situations here. So which is Lutwidge most likely to do?

You might think from the behavior of people in our mug example above that Lutwidge would go for the sure thing most often, and pay off the $50 immediately. Yet Kahneman and Tversky found quite the opposite—when people are faced with expected losses rather than gains, they're more likely to take chances than go with the sure thing (Kahneman & Tversky, 1979). So if Lutwidge was truly convinced that there was only a one in ten chance of him having to pay $500 as opposed to a sure chance he'd have to pay $50, he'll probably go for the gamble more often than not.

This tendency to take chances when faced with potential losses but to play it safe when faced with potential gains has all sorts of important implications for real life. For one thing, it suggests that the context of how we view decisions is extremely important. Most serious decisions in the world are what are known as approach-avoidance conflicts. They're situations where we stand to gain by taking a particular course of action, but we also stand to lose at the same time. The potential gains attract us and make us want to approach that action, but the potential losses repel us and make us want to avoid it. When faced with an approach-avoidance conflict, how we resolve it depends on how strongly the positive component attracts us as well as how strongly the negative component repels us. But if the positive and negative components are balanced, thus having more or less the same expected utility, then the issue of whether we focus on the chances of gain or the chances of loss become important. It becomes a matter of how we look at the decision, and from what angle, a process psychologists refer to as "framing."

Is the glass half empty or half full? Am I losing a daughter, or gaining a son-in-law? Is this the end of an era, or a new beginning? It's all in how you look at it. Frame most situations one way, and you focus on your losses; frame them another way, and you're focusing on your gains. And it matters which you do, because, as we've discussed above, we treat potential gains and losses quite differently.

Let's suppose that you're the mayor of a moderately-sized city, and you'd like to convince the City Council and the people to build a commercial port and support facilities in your currently unused harbor (Yes, I know most of you live in landlocked areas and don't have harbors. Just substitute the words "grain depot" for the words "commercial port" and the word "field" for "harbor" in that case). Compared to the status quo, your analysts calculate there's a 50-50 chance that this new harbor will double the income of most city residents. There's also a 50-50 chance that it will prevent a vast property tax increase that's scheduled for the next fiscal year by raising city income. But there's also a 50-50 chance that, after spending all the money to build a harbor and the roads to support it, shippers still won't move into it, and thus there's a chance that the money will go to waste and nothing will change. So we have the kind of situation Kahneman and Tversky tested. Residents have to choose between the sure thing, the income and the pending tax increase that they have now, and potential great gains that have a 50-50 chance of occurring.

So how should you sell your program to the people? Most people's first impulse would be to focus on the potential gain. "Vote to spend tax money on the port, and there's a 50-50 chance your property values and income will double." But as Kahneman and Tversky point out, when faced with a sure thing or a probabilistic gain, most people will stick with the sure thing, and vote your program down. Thus, if you really want public support for your port building plan, you'd want to focus instead on the penalties the people are currently suffering, and the probability those penalties will be reduced if the port is built. "Vote to spend tax money on the port, and there's a 50-50 chance the big tax increase next year can be avoided," is the message you'd want to send, because people will go for a probabilistic chance to avoid a loss rather than a sure loss.

The people in opposition to the building of the port, though, should focus on the iffiness of the potential gains, and how they already have a pretty good life without the port, because when faced with potential gains, people are more likely to keep the sure thing they already have than to trade it for a gain of equal expected utility but greater uncertainty. They should avoid talking about the chance of avoiding the tax increase entirely.

Now let's suppose that you're a pollster asking questions to determine public sentiment concerning the bill. You have a lot of leeway in how you ask your questions—you could emphasize the chances of eliminating the negative side of things, or you could emphasize the probability of making great gains. How you frame the question will have a big influence on how people answer. If you ask them, "Are you willing to change our currently decent town and take a chance on it becoming either a bustling economic powerhouse or a dying city saddled with a huge white elephant," they'll probably say they like the city the way it is and oppose the port proposal. But if you ask them, "Are you willing to spend money now so that you have a chance of avoiding the scheduled tax increase," many more people would be willing to take that chance than accept the sure increase.

When it comes to gains, then, people in general take the sure thing over a choice with equal expected utility but greater possible gain and greater risk. But if that's the case, why do people buy lottery tickets, bet on long shots when they play the ponies, or shoot craps? (Funny how I can't get away from that word.) These are all situations where they're trading a sure thing (money they already have) for a long chance at a large gain. Yet a lot of people buy lottery tickets or bet on other long-shots. Do these situations invalidate Kahneman and Tversky?

This is where things get interesting (I know it's hard to believe that this could get even more interesting, but bear with me). Human behavior is almost never simple and driven by just one motive or factor. We've been talking about the situation where the person considers the sure thing and the long shot to be of equal expected utility. But what if the person's evaluation of the expected utility of one of the items is inaccurate or biased compared to the evaluation of the other? I've mentioned before that humans have a tendency to categorize things that would be more accurately viewed as being on a continuum rather than in absolute, dichotomous groups. We do that with expected utility, too. When the odds of a situation get low enough, we start viewing them as, essentially, zero. As a consequence, an interesting thing happens when you start dealing with extremely small probabilities of extremely large gains. We start ignoring the odds entirely, and focus solely on what we stand to gain.

Say I give you a ticket that gives you one chance out of ten-thousand of winning $50,000. Then I offer to let you trade it for a ticket that gives you one chance out of twenty-thousand of winning

$100,000 instead. The expected utility of both these tickets is $5, so the offers are essentially equal. But because the odds of winning are very low in both cases, we treat our odds in both cases as being indistinguishable from zero. Having done so, we focus only on the size of the possible gain. Thus, in this situation, people take the option where they're more unlikely to win, but where the winnings are much bigger.

Looking at a practical application of this, let's suppose you're running a lottery, and you want people to play it as much as possible. Most state lotteries are 50-50 lotteries, which means that they guarantee that 50% of lottery proceeds will go into the prizes. (The other 50% of the proceeds are usually split between administration costs for the lottery itself and some worthy cause such as education that was used to sell people on the lottery to start with.) So if you buy a lottery ticket for a dollar, your expected utility is 50 cents.

That doesn't sound like such a great deal when we put it that way, does it? Compared to most games of chance in a gambling Mecca such as Las Vegas, it's not. For example, a roulette wheel normally contains the numbers 1 through 36 plus zero and double zero. Half the numbers are black, the other half red, and zero and double zero are green. Bet on black or red, and your odds of winning are a bit higher than 47%, because a bit less than 3% of the time the ball will land on green, and everyone loses but the house. But if you win, you get twice as much money back as you bet, so your expected value is double your winning percentage, or a bit less than 95%, which means you'll get, on the average, 95 cents for every dollar you bet. That's is quite a bit better than the 50 cents you'd get on the average for every dollar you put into the state lottery. Some places have roulette wheels with only a zero and no double zero, raising your expected utility to 97 cents for every dollar you spend. Wow, we're almost breaking even!

So you want people to bet on your lottery, yet the expected value for each dollar you spend is a miserable 50 cents. How do I sell that to the people? Would it be better to make the odds of winning greater, but the payoffs proportionately less, or make the odds of winning less but the payoffs proportionately greater?

If we look at Kahneman and Tversky's original research, we're dealing with potential gains. Given the choice of a sure thing or a chance at a better thing, people go with the sure thing. Thus, they'd keep their money rather than buy a lottery ticket. However, consider what happens if we make the prize very, very large, and the odds of winning very, very low, so low that we consider those odds pretty much zero. As we noted above, when people are faced with very, very long odds for both gains, as in the case of big jackpot lotteries, people reverse their patterns and chose the greater potential gain, even if the odds of getting that gain are much less. So if you're designing a lottery, you'll want at least one game where the odds against winning are quite fabulous, but the prize if one does win is fabulous, too. Once the odds of winning get low enough that it's a very low probability event, we're swayed only by potential winnings. Thus, the lottery that's giving away a hundred million dollars is far more attractive than one giving away a measily hundred thousand.

That's one of the reasons that many states have teamed up to create "Powerball" or "MegaMillions" lotteries—such giant lotteries create huge jackpots even while making it far less likely you'll actually win that jackpot. Such lotteries are popular, and get more popular the greater the prize becomes, even though the odds of winning are poorer than many other potential gambles. All we're focusing on is the size of the prize.

One has to consider one more factor in lottery play. Most people bet only small amounts of money on the lottery. For most, those amounts are a dollar or two--small enough as to be viewed as essentially nothing. If you view the amount you're using to buy the ticket as inconsequential, then your expected utility calculation becomes positive no matter how long the odds, because the cost to you is being viewed as essentially zero. The same is also true if you, like many lottery players, decide that you're getting enough entertainment value from the dollar you spent on the lottery just by being allowed to dream that you'll win for another week.

Next, let's turn to another situation where the odds of something happening are very low, and we also treat those odds of being equivalent to zero—situations involving very rare events occurring together.

Dealing with Incredibly Rare Coincidences and Very Rare Events

As I mentioned in the previous section, few people make much of a distinction between things that are highly improbable and things that are impossible. Once the odds of a particular occurrence get miniscule, we treat those odds as being zero, for all practical purposes. This means we often treat relatively rare events and very, very rare events as statistically equivalent and the odds of both as equivalent to zero. The net result is that we are often surprised when even mildly improbable things happen, as surprised as we would be if something impossible had happened.

But why shouldn't we be? I hear you ask. Especially when we're talking about things that are highly improbable, one in a million or one in a billion types of things? Shouldn't we be surprised when they happen? The answer is, surprisingly, no. That's because there is a world of difference between the likelihood that something is going to happen in a particular place at a particular time to a particular person, and the likelihood that it is going to happen at all to anyone, anywhere, at any time.

Let's go back to our example of the lottery. The odds of winning the jackpot in California's Superlotto Plus is currently slightly less than 1 in 47 million. That's a pretty low probability event, so low that I've never been even tempted to play the lottery. With odds like this, the chance that I'd win the lottery in a given week with a given ticket is so low that we'd all agree it's almost zero. But that's a lot different from the odds that anyone, anywhere will win the lottery this week. The odds of that depend on the number of ticket buyers, but they're reasonably good on any given week, and get more and more likely the more people play the lottery in a given week. Once we get into the tens of millions of tickets bought, the fact that someone will win becomes more likely than not.

What we're talking about here is the difference between the probability of a single event and the joint probability that any one of many, many events might happen. The odds any given person will win the lottery in any given week with a single play is miniscule, but the odds someone somewhere will win when many people play is much, much greater, and become greater the more people we're talking about.

Suppose that you get together with a group of 74 of your relatives and friends for a giant holiday bash at a local hotel. You have 75 assorted people gathered together in a sweaty mass, doing the chicken dance, or the hokey-pokey, or the Macarena, or the hustle, or whatever dance your people do. (Not much use of having a party unless you're going to get together in a sweaty mass.) What are the odds that two people in this perspiring pack share a birthday?

A lot of folks might conclude that the odds that any two of 75 people share a birthday are 74/365, or about one in five. After all, if each person in the room has a different birthday, then 74 of the 365 birthdays would be taken by the people in the room, and the odds your birthday would be one of those days would be only 74 out of 365. (We're not counting leap year birthdays here—as usual, you folks get lost in the shuffle). But those folks who think the odds of shared birthdays in a group this small are low would be seriously mistaken. The odds that at least 2 people share a birthday in a group of 75 is actually almost 100 percent.

Why are the odds of people sharing a birthday that much higher than we think? Because we're not talking about the odds that any single person will share a birthday with another. We're talking about the odds that any of the many, many combinations of two people will share any of the 365 possible birthdays. It's an important difference, akin to the difference between whether you, personally, will win the lottery and whether anyone will win the lottery. The odds you'll win the lottery are almost nil. (Sorry to rain on your parade). The odds that someone, somewhere will win the lottery are actually pretty good. Likewise, the odds you'll share your birthday with one of the people in the room isn't great, but the odds that some pair of people in the room will share some birthday are many times greater.

You don't even need that many people. Even if you've decided not to just throw money around like it was free and are having a much smaller bash in your back yard with just 22 other people and you serving as your own DJ, odds are better than 50-50 that two of those sweaty, booty-shaking people share a birthday. That's why, although we're often surprised to find that people in a group share a birthday, we shouldn't be. It's actually quite common.

You have to consider the difference between the odds that a particular thing will happen to a particular person in a particular place at a particular time and the odds that something will happen to someone somewhere at some time when you are judging the improbable coincidences of the world as well. For example, on March 7, 2002, a pair of identical twin brothers in Raahe, Finland, were killed only hours apart when they were hit by trucks in individual accidents while riding their bicycles. There was no apparent connection between the accidents. In fact, the second twin was not aware of the first's accident because the police had not yet informed the family and the two did not live together. The story was reported all over the world because of how unlikely it was overall. And I'll admit that it's mind-bogglingly unlikely. What are the odds, you ask, that a pair of twins would die from the same cause at about the same time while doing the same thing? Well, they're not very high, I'll grant you that. We're probably talking about something that has only a one in several billion chance of happening. Maybe even something with a one in several hundred billion chance of occurring. So the odds that it would happen to these two individuals isn't great. (Although odds are greater than they might first appear. Biking as a way to get around is much more common in Raahe than in the average American city, and bad weather conditions make the odds of multiple accidents on a given day more likely).

Still, there's a world of difference between something being unlikely and it being impossible. That difference is simply that impossible things never happen, but unlikely things happen every day. Even though the odds that a particular pair of twins would die of the same unlikely sort of accident on the same day is very, very low, the odds that something very unlikely would happen in a given day to someone somewhere in the world is actually fairly high. If it hadn't been a pair of twins dying of the same cause in separate accidents on the same day, it would have been a pair of high school sweethearts rediscovering each other because they were both hostages in a bank takeover, or a man spearing a shark that turned out to have a class ring from his old high school in its stomach, or some other ridiculously unlikely thing. On any given day, a number of extremely unlikely things are likely to happen, because there are just so many people in the world doing so many things that at least one unlikely thing happening is a virtual certainty. And every year or so, something absurdly unlikely is likely to happen. Look at it this way—if the odds of something happening are a billion to one, it isn't likely to happen to you or any other given person—but chances are almost certain that it will happen to at least one of the 7 billion people in the world today, and on the average it will happen to around 7 of them on a given day.

People often feel compelled to try to "explain" why events of vanishingly small likelihood happen. Often, they'll invoke vast, complex conspiracies to explain coincident events. "Lutwidge just happens to call in sick on the day that the gas explosion blew up his office building, even though he's never missed a day! What are the odds of that? He must have known it was going to happen!" "Yeah, and didn't he work in that other town where they had the gas explosion in the factory?" "That can't be a coincidence! He must be blowing up buildings!"

Other times, people suggest that events that are very unusual or unlikely must have been the result of supernatural powers. "Lutwidge's doctor said he was riddled with tumors, and only had 6 months to live. But after he visited that voodoo shrine, they tested him and the tumors were gone, and he's healthy as a horse! The voodoo must have cured him!"

What people don't consider is that, although a particular series of events is unlikely, the odds that any unlikely event of any kind will occur in a given place is actually very high over a several month period. It's unlikely that the one day Lutwidge finally missed work would be the day a gas leak blew up his building, but some unlikely event of some kind is likely to happen in our vicinity every so often, because billions of things happen every day. Yes, only one in millions of patients suddenly have their immune systems surge and destroy advanced cancers, but it does happen. We really don't need to invoke fanciful explanations when it does. People will say, "But what were the chances that Lutwidge would get better?" What they should be asking is, "What are the chances someone, somewhere, would get better when they were in his condition?" Those chances are much more likely, and thus not surprising at all, nor in need of explanation.

(By the way, why do we use the metaphor "healthy as a horse" to describe someone who's in good health, and "sick as a dog" to describe someone who's ill? Horses are actually fairly delicate creatures, finicky about food and possessing of long legs vulnerable to fracture. Are they a better example of the epitome of health than dogs? What about other animals? Cows are pretty placid, sturdy beasts that can eat almost anything with cellulose in it and survive. Why don't we say, "Healthy as a cow? And why, "sick as a dog?" Dogs can live outside in terrible climates, and thrive on half-rotting meat and garbage. Are they really the epitome of illness? Raccoons are the most common carriers of rabies. Shouldn't we say, "Sick as a raccoon?")

Back to our discussion. When Lutwidge stopped being sick as a raccoon and fought off his cancer, this wasn't an impossible event, just an improbable one. It really doesn't need explanation—now and then cancer spontaneously remits even when very advanced. It doesn't happen often, so it's not likely to happen to a given person. But it's very likely to happen to someone, given the millions of people who have cancer.

We're really creating mysteries here that aren't mysteries at all. By underestimating the likelihood of rare events, we ensure that rare events, when they do occur, will shock and surprise us. People often say in cases like Lutwidge's that science can't explain his recovery, but in truth, science has no trouble explaining his recovery at all—his immune system rallied, recognized the cancers as intruder cells, and engaged in a massive attack on those cells, eradicating them. It doesn't happen often, but it does happen. What people really mean when they say that science can't explain his recovery is that science doesn't address why it was Lutwidge in particular who recovered. But that's not due to science's inadequacy, but because the question being asked isn't a valid one. When one out of 47 million people win the lottery, it makes no sense to ask "why him?" Someone was likely to, and if it hadn't been him, it would have been someone else.

Engineers, in fact, argue that it's good practice to anticipate even extremely rare events, expect them, and to the degree we can, plan for them. This attitude is embodied in the very famous "Murphy's Law." Murphy's Law is usually expressed as "Whatever can go wrong will go wrong," but is sometimes expanded to, "Whatever can go wrong will go wrong, and at the worst possible time." It was named after a technician at Edwards Air Force Base in the 1960's, Captain Edward A. Murphy who, upon discovering a device was wired improperly, commented about the technician who wired it, "if there is any way to do it wrong, he'll find it." His project manager, Dr. John Paul Stapp, began referring to the inevitability of everything going wrong sooner or later as "Murphy's Law," and the name stuck (Spark, 2006).

Murphy's Law reminds engineers and planners that we should not dismiss a risk or omit planning for an outcome just because that outcome is rare, nor can we use that as an excuse when things fail.

It's not likely that the particular new bridge you're designing will ever be lined with large trucks from end to end in all four lanes during hurricane force winds. But the odds that someone's engineering project somewhere will face such an unlikely combination of things going wrong is quite high in a given time period, and there are lots and lots of such projects, so unless we want to experience a lot of disasters caused by unlikely events, it's best if we plan for the worst, at least up to a point. Still, at some point we have to accept that some very rare events will strike now and then, and there's no way of anticipating when.

Humans are terrific pattern recognizers, but we don't do well in estimating probabilities, or in judging the likelihood of rare events. This makes us easy targets for fear-mongerers with an agenda of their own. It also drives us to allocate our resources in less than ideal ways. In turn, we're driven to believe in artificial mysteries that "science can't explain." We're such good pattern matchers that we look for patterns when they aren't actually there, and for explanations for things that simply happened. Then we invent all sorts of improbable mechanisms and unseen forces and all manner of conspiracies to explain these rare events, because we're unable to accept that events that are rare nonetheless do happen, and there are so many such possibilities that even events that are exceedingly rare by themselves happen frequently when all such possibilities are considered together.

Now what are the odds I can get the conspiracy theorists to actually understand and accept that information?

References:

Kahneman, D., & Tversky, A. (1979) Prospect theory: An analysis of decision under risk. *Econometrica, 47*, 263-291.

Laumann, E., and Michael, R. (Eds.) (2001) . Sex, Love, and Health in America: Private Choices and Public Policies. Chicago:University of Chicago Press.

National Weather Service (2010). *Medical Aspects of lightning*. Retrieved from http://www.lightningsafety.noaa.gov/medical.htm

US Department of Transportation Pipeline and Hazardous Materials Safety Administration (2010). Hazmat Safety: A comparison of Risk. Retrieved from http://www.phmsa.dot.gov/portal/site/PHMSA/menuitem.ebdc7a8a7e39f2e55cf2031050248a0c/?vgnextoid=8524adbb3c60d110VgnVCM1000009ed07898RCRD&vgnextchannel=4f347fd9b896b110VgnVCM1000009ed07898RCRD&vgnextfmt=print

Spark, N. T. (2006) *A history of murphy's law*. Los Angeles: Periscope Film.

Chapter 3: We Hold this Truth to be Self-evident: We aren't all Created Equal

We hold these truths to be self-evident, that *all men are created equal...*
Thomas Jefferson, *The Declaration of Independence*

I swim against the tide because I like to annoy. Carlos Ruiz Zafón, Spanish language novelist.

I don't use drugs, my dreams are frightening enough. M. C. Escher, mathematician and perspective artist.

Philosophers, Novelists, and the Founding Fathers

Back in 1690, scholar/philosopher John Locke wrote a treatise entitled *An Essay Concerning Human Understanding.* (Locke, 1996). In it, he proposed that humans were born as "tabula rasa," or "blank slates," ready to be written on by the hand of experience. Newborns were neither inclined toward good nor inclined toward evil at birth. Instead, they became inclined toward whatever they were taught as a result of their experiences with the world. The position Locke took in proposing that children were tabula rasa was in opposition to the position of some of his predecessors, such as philosopher Thomas Hobbes (Hobbes, 1997). Hobbes had argued, earlier in that century, that humans were by nature inherently selfish and evil. He further proposed that life without society to control human nature would of necessity be "solitary, poor, nasty, brutish, and short." The Hobbesian point of view was echoed in modern times in that perennial favorite of junior high literature assignments, William Golding's *Lord of the Flies* (Golding, 1999). In his novel, Golding proposed that if you leave the children alone without the benefit of the moderating effects of society, savagery will prevail, and those who use logic and reason will end up with their heads skewered on sharpened sticks.

Locke, though, took issue with Hobbes' thoroughly pessimistic view, suggesting that children weren't inherently evil, wild creatures who needed to be civilized, but were instead simply empty plates, ready to be filled up with whatever their culture served them in the grand smorgasbord of life experience. Locke's view, in turn, had a startlingly strong influence on the Founding Fathers of America. Benjamin Franklin, John Adams, and, most of all, Thomas Jefferson were well versed in the writings of Locke, and their writings about human equality and about what constituted just government reflected their appreciation of his work. It's an easy jump from the idea that we're born tabula rasa to the concept that, therefore, all humans start on an equal footing, or, in Jefferson's words, "all men are created equal."

Americans are great believers in this principle. We're all created equal. Given the opportunity, we can make of ourselves anything we want, provided our society doesn't oppress us, take advantage of us, or otherwise hold us back, and provided our society provides us with the tools we need to learn to become productive citizens. You're born with the same basic faculties as everyone else, this is the land of opportunity, and given a just government in a free society, we'd all have the same chance to make something of ourselves. (There's an intriguing corollary to this reasoning as well—if we all are created equal and have equal opportunity, then if you haven't made as much of yourself as others, it must also be your fault.)

But Locke wasn't the only philosopher to influence the Founding Fathers. Franklin, Jefferson, and the other revolutionaries who were fluent in French also were aware of the writings of another philosopher somewhat more their contemporary, Jean Jacques Rousseau. Rousseau took a position very much in opposition to those of both Hobbes and Locke, arguing that newborn children were neither inherently evil beasts not blank slates, but rather were inclined to avoid causing and witnessing suffering, and thus were driven by empathy to be innately decent people. English readers of Rousseau immediately related Rousseau's view to an earlier idea, that of the *noble savage.*

It's hard, really, for the average modern reader to relate to the idea of the noble savage. You have to be in the mindset of 17th and 18th century Europeans. By the 1600s Europeans had sailed all over the globe in their leaky wooden sailing ships, munching as they sailed on wormy, almost inedible bread and salted meat so tough you could chew it for hours. Most of the places they went, with the exception of a few odd, unpopulated corners of the globe like Pitcairn Island and the Galapagos Islands, they found other humans already living, humans who did not share European culture or speak European languages, and who often did not have technology such as iron working or gunpowder. Being untouched by European culture, (and often not completely welcoming to these invaders from elsewhere) these people were immediately relegated to the European category "savages."

But, to the Europeans' joint surprise, many of these people were nonetheless good folks, people you could do business with, people who seemed to be reasonably moral, in short, people of a level of integrity that rivaled that of some of the more "civilized"

Europeans. It surprised the Europeans mightily that they could be hard-working people of integrity and still not have been made that way by the supposedly morally superior cultures of Europe. The myth of the noble savage arose out of this perceived conundrum—the idea that some people were inherently noble, and if not perverted by their experience or their societies would develop into noble, if savage, people. Rousseau likened the development of humans, including that of the so-called noble savages, to the development of a growing flower. Just as a flower will unfold according to its nature if not prevented from doing so by local climate conditions, humans will develop according to their own morally positive inclinations unless prevented from doing so by society.

Of course, that doesn't mean that all people had the potential to be noble savages. Remember, we're talking about France prior to the French Revolution of 1789-1799. Wealthy people such as Rousseau and the educated audience who would have been reading his writings were primarily people of "noble blood." They easily accepted the idea that some human beings, and even some family lines of human beings, were superior to others, and that superiority was something inborn.

If you want to see an example of an author who not only swallowed Rousseau's argument hook, line, and sinker, but threatened to swallow the fishing pole as well, you can't do much better than Edgar Rice Burroughs, author of the *Tarzan of the Apes* series (Burroughs, 2008). Tarzan is born of noble parents, John and Alice Clayton, who also happen to be nobility--Lord and Lady Greystoke of England, and his birth makes him heir to that title. Unfortunately, the timing of this birth isn't optimal, because it comes shortly after Lord Greystoke and his pregnant wife are shipwrecked off the coast of Africa. They name their new infant John after his father, but almost immediately after the Greystoke heir is born, his parents are attacked and killed by "killer apes." (Killer apes were an Edgar Rice Burroughs fiction—no actual, existing ape groups are nearly as blood thirsty as those proposed in the Tarzan books. Nor are there any apes other than the relatively placid and gentle gorillas that are as large as those Burroughs described. The killer apes in the Burroughs story were probably modeled after some of the more beastly humans of the world).

One of the "killer apes" of Burroughs' creation, having just lost her own baby to some ape analogue of crib death, scoops up the orphaned human infant and provides him with nourishment and protection as he grows up. The apes also possess a primitive language ability, and they dub the infant "Tarzan," which apparently means "white skin." Although possessing language, the apes do not possess human morals and cannot teach them to young Tarzan. Those morals, according to Burroughs, arose internally in young Tarzan, a product of his "noble blood." As he matures, Tarzan supposedly senses instinctively the things that are moral and immoral. For example, when the ape tribe kills some local humans, young Tarzan knows instantly that it would be immoral to eat the victims, even as his fellow ape tribe members are digging in with abandon, relish, and considerable ape-like growling. Ultimately, when as a young man Tarzan saves a hunting party including the cousin who has taken his rightful place as Lord Greystoke, he is taught French and the manners of a gentleman, and ultimately turns out to be more moral and to have more integrity than many of the more "civilized" characters he has to confront. Rousseau would have found this outcome completely plausible—Tarzan did, after all, come from superior human stock. It's not an outcome that either Hobbes or Locke would have anticipated, however.

So by the time of the founding of the new American Republic, we had three completely contrasting views of humanity: The view of

Hobbes, who saw us as inherently prone to evil unless compelled by society to be good, the view of Rousseau, who saw most of us as inherently prone to good (as long as we have good genes and aren't corrupted by society), and the view of Locke, who saw us as blank slates, ready to be written on by that same society, and thus neither inherently good nor inherently evil. Perhaps because most Americans were laborers and farmers of peasant origin who had recently thrown off the yoke of a hereditary ruling class, the bulk of Americans were more inclined to believe the views of Locke and Hobbes than that of Rousseau. Many of these early settlers were Puritans, and Puritans were strongly influenced by Hobbes. Locke's message also resonated with the Puritans, especially his suggestions that anyone had the potential to be anything, if enough effort were put into generating the right experiences for them, and if the person worked at it hard enough.

But many of the Founding Fathers were wealthy men, people who employed (and sometimes enslaved) many other people. We shouldn't be surprised that some parts of Rousseau's message resonated with them as well, at least the idea that some people might have an edge on others in ability or in other positive human qualities. That peculiar institution involved in the election of the president, the Electoral College, probably owes its existence to this attitude. The people could vote directly for lesser officials, but the vote for the supreme leader of the republic would be made by lesser leaders of that republic, people who had demonstrated superior political acumen to the point where they could convince others to vote for them as their representatives

All three of these views of humanity continue to thrive in America right up to the present day. But Locke's message had a particular influence on American psychology, because his views resonated with John Watson, whose behaviorism dominated American Psychology for 50 years, from the early 1910s into the 1960s

(Watson, 1930). Behaviorism is the branch of psychology that tried to explain behavior by reference only to the stimuli that each organism experienced, and to the responses that occurred to those stimuli, discounting any other influences as being of only minor note. Like Locke, behaviorists argued that children were simply what their experiences made of them. It was Watson who said, echoing Locke,

Give me a dozen healthy infants, well-formed, and my own specified world to bring them up in and I'll guarantee to take any one at random and train him to become any type of specialist I might select – doctor, lawyer, artist, merchant-chief and, yes, even beggar-man and thief, regardless of his talents, penchants, tendencies, abilities, vocations, and race of his ancestors.

You might wonder why Watson so adamantly rejected genetic influences on human beings' behaviors, and focused only on experience in childhood as the major determiner of our fates. Often times we can directly link an individual's behaviors to peculiarities of their own childhood experiences. Sigmund Freud, for example, was the product of an indulgent, loving mother and a more emotionally distant, less involved father. (This was largely responsible for Freud's belief in the Oedipal Complex, an issue you can read about in Chapter 2 of the companion volume in this series, *Psychology in Plain English*).

So what sort of childhood did John Watson have that would encourage embracing the "blank slate" view? By his own reports, an extremely non-promising one. Watson was born in Texas, but his father left the family soon after and moved in with a pair of other women who lived in the same town, abandoning his wife and son. His mother subscribed to what many would consider abusive parenting practices, including lengthy and humiliating corporal punishments. Young John appears to have been an unruly lad, and was reportedly involved in several juvenile arrests, some of which involved use of firearms. But he was also extremely bright, and despite his impoverished and abusive upbringing, entered college early, worked his way through it and graduate school, and secured a professorship at the University of Chicago and later, Johns Hopkins University. He credited his educational experiences with his success, discounting genetic influences from his less than academically stellar parents (Buckley, 1989).

Yet one could just as easily turn Watson's argument on its head, and argue that he was able to grow beyond and overcome an extremely impoverished and less than ideal environment precisely because he possessed superior genetic gifts. Watson would be what psychologists now call a "resilient child," a child who shakes off devastating environmental conditions to become a decent and functional person regardless. Others placed in his circumstances might have turned out very differently indeed. So what could have made Watson different, if not his genetic endowments?

Genetic Influences on Behavior

All of this raises the question of just how genes influence behaviors. How can the arrangements of the bases in your DNA result in you acting differently from someone with different arrangements? DNA, after all, only specifies how to create the proteins that build our bodies and the proteins that serve functions in their operation. How does that translate into behavior?

There are quite a few pathways through which genes influence behavior. In the most direct path, genes can create structures that directly trigger behaviors. For example, normal humans are born with a built-in reflex to breathe when carbon dioxide levels build up in the bloodstream. Carbon dioxide combines with our blood fluids to form carbonic acid. This changes the pH of the blood, making it more acidic, and neurons that connect to blood vessels react to this more acidic state by sending signals to the brain stem, which in turn stimulates an increase in respiration rate. Because genes made the structures that then create the behavior of breathing when carbon dioxide levels rise, we can say breathing is a genetically coded behavior, what many call a reflex, and what psychologists call a "fixed response pattern" or a "fixed action pattern."

Humans have their share of such fixed response patterns, or reflexes. Actually, we probably have more than our share of them. This sometimes comes as a surprise to beginning psychology students. Humans are more capable of logic and reason than other animals, and have a much larger forebrain than other animals. This leads us to assume that, therefore, our instincts and reflexes must be fewer in number than is the case for other animals. But William James, the original founder of American psychology and a powerful influence on it for decades, once pointed out that, the larger the brain, the more space there is to hide reflexes, and the more complex those reflexes can be (James, 1890). A brain consisting of just 40 neurons would have only limited potential for reflexes, because there's only so much such a simple brain could do. But our brains, with perhaps as many as 100 billion neurons, would have room for many, many reflexes indeed.

Still, most genetically-influenced behaviors aren't reflexes or fixed response patterns, waiting to be triggered by specific stimuli. Most genes have influence on behavior in another, less direct way—they create structures that make some behaviors more comfortable than others. Because of that comfort advantage, people are then more likely to do that behavior than some alternative. These sorts of genetically influenced behaviors tend to be called "instincts," a word referring to things we're inclined to do because of genes, but aren't compelled to do. Let's say, for example, that a child is born with a particularly underactive reticular formation. The reticular formation is deep within the hind brain, and, among its other functions, it controls our overall alertness and awareness. Because of genetic factors, this child's reticular formation responds to stimulation much less than most other children's, and thus it takes a lot of stimulation to get this child interested, and an almost insane level to send this child into alarm mode. For such a child, quiet, soothing environments would be more boring and uncomfortable than for most people, and noisy, dangerous ones might actually be comfortably stimulating, even pleasurable exciting. Such a child might, from the very beginning of locomotion, seek out such raucous, even dangerous environments, or create such an environment if none could be found. Yet a different child, with an overactive reticular formation, might find even the smallest hint of danger to be uncomfortably alarming. Such a child might avoid even the slightest stimulation, preferring calm, quiet, predictable surroundings.

In situations such as this, genes aren't directly influencing behavior as they are with reflexes. They simply make body and brain structures that make some behaviors more comfortable than others. Thus, the connection between genes and behavior is a bit more tenuous than it is with reflexes. We're not forced to go the direction our genetically-influenced bodily structures are pointing us by making certain behaviors more comfortable. We're just inclined to do the more comfortable thing unless other factors intrude. For example, I often ask students in my classes when we reach this point in the discussion to put down their pens and hold their arms straight out in front of them, parallel with the ground. Go ahead and do it yourself—I'll wait.

Got your arm in position? Good. Now look at your palm. Is it facing up, or down? Pretty much all of my students will hold their arms with the palms of their hands facing down, and I bet you did, too. The structures of our arms make it mildly uncomfortable to hold our arms out with the palm facing up. Go ahead and try it—you'll see what I mean.

So your tendency to hold your arm with the palm down when you extend it is genetically influenced. But it's only **influenced**, by genes, it's not **controlled** by them. If I were to say, "Here, I have $20 for you," those hands would flip over before you could say "free money." Your instinct might push you one way, but it's a fairly easy instinct to oppose. (By the way, you can put your arm down now. I'm not really handing out real money because I haven't yet become ridiculously wealthy, nor have I lost my mind.)

Most of the genetic influences on us are of this sort—general propensities or instincts rather than reflexes. Thus, most human genetic influences don't compel us, they're simply inclinations to do something as opposed to something else. We can go along with those inclinations, or we can oppose them. Genetics isn't destiny. It's one of the reasons that identical twins are never identical in behavior, even for genetically-influenced traits, despite their almost identical genetic endowments. (Identical twins are only almost identical. Yes, they both originate from the same zygote, so they initially start with the same genes. But mutations inevitably occur during development, and thus they never end up quite identical, even in genetic structure. If one of those mutations is a particularly influential one, they can end up quite different in appearance. And even if no mutations occurred, identical twins would still not be identical. Differences in their environments starting in the uterus mean that they don't grow quite identically,. They'll have similar but not identical fingerprints, for example, because fingerprints are a combination of genetic propensities and fluid flow in the uterus.)

Then we get to the influence of the environment after birth. Identical twins are usually structured so similarly that they're often inclined the same directions. But we don't have to go the direction our structures incline us. Most of us tend to "go with the flow" most of the time, accepting the inclinations our bodies prefer. But a given twin might decide instead to "swim upstream," actively opposing what his or her body finds comfortable. Suppose we have two identical twins who are born with overactive reticular formations, as described above. One might do what's comfortable, and seek quiet, predictable friends and surroundings. The other, though, might see his constant alarm reactions as a weakness, and work hard to overcome that weakness. He might deliberately insert himself in alarm-inducing surroundings, and set out to learn ways to control his alarm reactions as well as endeavoring to get used to loud stimuli. With enough experience, he might become a very different person from his cowering, easily frightened brother.

The bottom line is that we have genetic tendencies that make some behaviors more comfortable than others, and those tendencies thus incline us to certain behaviors. So where do our genetic tendencies tend to pop up the most? One of the major genetic and biological differences between people involves the production and functioning of neurotransmitters.

Neurotransmitters are special chemicals created by neurons. They're necessitated by the fact that neurons in humans and animals seldom actually touch each other. Because they don't touch, a given neuron can't signal the next neuron electrically, nor can a neuron signal a muscle to contract or an organ to function electrically. Instead, the axon terminals of one neuron tend to be separated from the dendrites of others by a microscopic gap known as a synapse. To send signals across that synapse, neurons use neurotransmitters, special chemicals that the axon terminals release. When an electrical signal comes down a neuron and reaches the ends of it, or the axon terminals, neurotransmitter molecules are driven out, where they fly across the synapse, attaching to dendrites of other neurons and trying to coax them to fire and send the signal on, or attaching to receptors in muscles or organs and making them function.

There are more than 40 different neurotransmitters used by the human neural system. Different parts of the brain and different types of neurons use different combinations of them. More relevant to our discussion, the overall level of production of each neurotransmitter, the rate at which they're broken down, and our tendency to react to each are all things that vary from person to person and can be affected by genetic factors. As a result, brain functioning and nervous system functioning can vary dramatically from person to person. In the next section, we'll talk about variations in production and response to some of these neurotransmitters and how they might contribute to all of us being somewhat less than equal right from the moment we're born.

Neurotransmitter Variations in Humans

We'll start by looking at a very important neurotransmitter, dopamine. Dopamine is important to movement and muscle control, and it plays roles in learning and reasoning in the frontal lobes. In this discussion, though, we're going to focus on the roles dopamine plays in the brain's reward system. Feelings of reward in humans appear to involve processing in sections of the prefrontal lobes of the brain, and stimulation of activity in the **nucleus accumbens**. Rewarding experiences such as food when we're hungry, water when we're thirsty, sex pretty much all the time, and possibly even domination of others and aggression toward others appear to involve release of dopamine in these areas. High levels of dopamine in the nucleus accumbens, especially, appear to be associated with visceral pleasure. That's why it should not be at all surprising that many drugs that give pleasure stimulate dopamine release in the frontal lobes and the nucleus accumbens. Included in this group of highly pleasurable drugs are most stimulants, such as cocaine, nicotine, and methamphetamine, but also sedatives such as alcohol, and even some odd duck drugs such as marijuana.

People appear to vary in their levels of dopamine production, in their responsiveness to dopamine, and in how readily they break down and dispose of dopamine when it becomes elevated. The interactions between these factors are often complex and sometimes contradictory. We're going to take a look at just one such factor—how readily the person can break down dopamine and dispose of it.

One of the factors in the breakdown and regulation of dopamine in humans and animals is the production of the enzyme monoamine oxidase, generally referred to as MAO. MAO floats in the synapses between neurons, breaking down all the neurotransmitters in the monoamine class, including dopamine, and thus preventing them from accumulating in the synapse and continuously stimulating neurons to fire. Some people seem to produce much higher amounts of MAO than others. Those who produce high amounts of MAO readily break down dopamine when it is released. Those who produce low amounts of MAO, on the other hand, are slow to break down dopamine, and thus dopamine can have more powerful and lingering positive effects for such people (Zuckerman, 1994).

Research into the differences between those who produce high amounts of MAO and those who produce low amounts have found that those who produce low amounts tend to be sensation seekers—people who find powerful sensations and dangerous pursuits and activities rewarding. Those who produce high amounts of MAO, on the other hand, appear to prefer lower levels of stimulation, and find dangerous pursuits and activities to be far less inviting. It appears that those who produce low amounts of MAO experience much more powerful positive feelings to stimulation, because dopamine tends to surge to high levels in places like the nucleus accumbens. Those who produce high amounts of MAO, by contrast, quickly break down the extra dopamine released by high levels of stimulation, and thus find the overall experience less rewarding.

Now consider what happens when people from each of these groups snort cocaine. Cocaine raises dopamine and several companion neurotransmitters sky high throughout the body. This generally results in great pleasure signals from the nucleus accumbens, and is one of the reasons many people find cocaine highly pleasurable and yearn for the opportunity to take it again. But reactions to cocaine would be very different for those with low levels of MAO and those with high levels of MAO. Those who produce low levels of MAO would experience more prolonged periods of dopamine elevation as a result of snorting cocaine, and also would experience greater elevations of dopamine as well. Those who produce high levels of MAO, on the other hand, would experience lower peak dopamine levels, and the effects would also be much shorter in duration. So those who produce high levels of MAO probably would not find cocaine nearly as pleasurable as those who produce low levels of MAO—in fact, if their MAO production was high enough, they may not find the experience of taking cocaine that much more pleasurable than the experiences in their lives they already enjoy. As a result, they also may find that the other effects of the drug (such as racing heart rates, ridiculous blood pressure levels, and serious paranoia) aren't outweighed by the pleasurable effects of the drug. Such a person would probably find that they could take or leave cocaine, and not be strongly drawn to it. But those who have low MAO levels may reach heights of ecstasy on cocaine that other people never feel. Such people may find cocaine to be just what the doctor ordered, raising their dopamine levels in a way that no other life experience can duplicate.

Sigmund Freud himself was one of several physicians who experimented with the anesthetic and stimulant qualities of cocaine back when it was first introduced to Europe as a new drug. He suggested it as a treatment for morphine addiction, and he also tried small quantities of the drug on himself, noting that he seemed mentally sharper and clearer when using it, and that it increased his circulation and brought color to his cheeks. He apparently didn't feel powerful cravings for it, nor did he experience the powerful reward feelings that drive many to use the drug. He commented favorably on the drug's stimulant effects in articles, and he even prescribed it for several patients before negative reports of the drug's addictiveness began coming out. It's very possible that Freud produced high levels of MAO, and thus the increase in dopamine levels and the consequent pleasure caused by that increase wasn't that great, or that his base dopamine levels were high enough from his normal life experiences that the increase caused by cocaine wasn't that much more pleasurable.

(You can make a good case for the latter argument. The personality traits that are associated with high levels of dopamine release as a normal state of affairs include many qualities Freud had in spades, including strong levels of self-confidence, feelings of grandeur, and complete assurance that one is right. Students sometimes ask me if it's true that Freud was drug-addicted, and I respond that he was. But it wasn't cocaine Freud was addicted to, it was good old-fashioned nicotine. Freud was mad about cigars, and smoked then almost constantly. It was this addiction that ultimately caused his serious health decline in later life and his death as well.)

Another biological quality that might incline some people to be more prone to using drugs than others is the tendency toward excessive alertness and high levels of anxiety. Alertness and anxiety are both tied to the neurotransmitter norepinephrine. When your norepinephrine levels are low, you tend to be slow-thinking, fuzzy-headed, and unambitious. When norepinephrine levels are are elevated, you're aware, sharp, and capable of fast, clear thinking. But elevate levels even higher than that, and we start getting edgy, anxious, paranoid, and fearful. We can't control our darting thoughts and our worries, we can't sleep, and we can't even relax. Most folks find that increasing norepinephrine is pleasurable up to a point, then less pleasurable and downright uncomfortable if we increase it past that point.

It's a reciprocal relationship, too. That is, high levels of norepinephrine make you anxious, stressed, and uncomfortable, but having many demands on you also raises your norepinephrine levels. Thus, having high levels of norepinephrine raises your anxiety levels, but being placed in stressful situations raises your norepinephrine as well. Raising your norepinephrine levels is one of the effects of triggering the body's fight or flight reaction, something that happens naturally when you're in threatening conditions. Very threatening events result in uncomfortably high levels of norepinephrine, and thus uncomfortable levels of anxiety.

So let's say you have a lot of stress in your work lives—lots of demands on you, excessive pressures, and worries galore. Your norepinephrine levels have been pushed up by your body's response to what appears to be a continuous emergency situation, to the point where they reach uncomfortable levels. So what do you want to do as soon as work is over?

For most people, that's obvious. You want to go somewhere quiet and let your emergency reactions calm down. You'll be attracted to your quiet home, or to a quiet corner bar where you can sit with other quiet people. You may also be attracted to imbibe in alcohol, one of the world's oldest and most effective sedatives. Drinking has a particular attraction in this scenario, because it increases effects of another neurotransmitter, gamma-amino-butyric acid, or GABA. GABA is an inhibitory neurotransmitter, a neurotransmitter that reduces the likelihood of neural firing. GABA tends to oppose the effects of excitatory neurotransmitters such as norepinephrine. Reducing uncomfortably high norepinephrine levels allows us to calm our nerves and slow our uncontrolled, rapid thoughts, and thus can be very rewarding after a hard day at a stressful job.

Now let's say that you show more than the usual norepinephrine production when you're placed in conditions that threaten or challenge you. As a result, you're hyper alert even in normal conditions, and when placed under pressure that alertness quickly climbs to discomfort and then extreme anxiety. For such a person, sedatives like alcohol are even more rewarding, because the symptoms they remove are just that much more excessive, unpleasant, and disturbing. The attraction of alcohol to people with a tendency to overproduce norepinephrine would be much greater and use of the drug much harder to resist than for people whose level of production is more normal.

Is there evidence that some people have a built-in biological tendency to become more readily addicted to drugs like alcohol than others? Absolutely. For starters, numerous studies have found that the children of alcoholics are at far greater risk to alcoholism themselves, even when they are adopted into other families and are not aware of the alcoholism of their parents. Studies also suggest that those prone to alcoholism may be prone to over-alertness as well. In one study, adult children of alcoholics who had chosen to abstain from alcohol use were asked to stand as still as possible balanced on just one foot. Sensitive motion detectors measured their overall body sway, and compared it to the body sway levels of peers who did not have alcoholic parents but who also did not drink. The children of alcoholics were found to sway more overall than those of non-alcoholics, suggesting a tendency to overcorrect small body movements. After having a single drink, children of non-alcoholics swayed more than before. But children of alcoholics actually swayed less after having a drink. The alcohol in the drink apparently calmed down their over-functioning systems (Schuckit, 1998).

Bottom line? It's probably much easier for some people to become addicted to alcohol than others, because we aren't created equal. For those with normal norepinephrine levels, alcohol has mildly pleasurable calming effects as well as a providing a mild sense of well-being. But for those with excessive norepinephrine production, it gives much stronger relief from their constant arousal and anxiety, a relief that they may come to crave on a daily basis. In a sense, these people are self-medicating. They're treating unpleasant physical symptoms with a drug that's readily available.

Reactivity and Babies

It's not just drug addiction tendencies that separate people genetically from other people. Other researchers have focused on reactivity, our tendency to show strong physiological reactions to stimuli. Jerome Kagan spent a number of years examining the reactions of 5-month-olds to having a mobile shaken in front of their faces. The reaction to this experience varies widely from child to child. Some babies react wildly, thrashing arms and legs, vocalizing, and even bursting into tears. At the other end of the extreme, there are babies who show a very different reaction, staring placidly and even cheerfully at the array of items dancing on strings in front of them. Kagan has found that babies who react very strongly to the mobile at 5 months tend to become shy, retiring, and even fearful toddlers and preschoolers. Those who are calm and relaxed while being assaulted by a legion of dancing toys directly in their faces tend to be far more cheerful and outgoing in the years that follow (Kagan and Fox, 2006).

Kagan's work actually is an extension of temperament research that traces back to the work of Chess and Thomas (Chess & Thomas, 1984, Thomas and Chess, 1977). Chess and Thomas examined a large group of newborns, discovering three prominent temperament categories: easy babies, difficult babies, and slow-to-warm-up babies. Easy babies they described as being generally positive in their reactions to things and people, regular in habits, and easily adaptable to new things and change. They're easygoing and happy most of the time. It's obvious why this category was named as it was—easy babies probably make their parents wonder what all the fuss is concerning the difficulty of taking care of babies.

Difficult babies, on the other hand, wake and sleep unpredictably, and eat unpredictably as well. They are intense and negative in most of their reactions. They don't like new things, new people, or new foods, and they let parents know at the tops of their tiny little lungs. They're more easily irritated and they're loud about it. They do eventually adapt to new things, but the adjustment process is longer than with easy babies. You have one of these, and you might seriously reconsider your plans of having multiple children (if such a thing is even possible when you have a baby in the house who wakes up screaming at all hours of the night).

Slow-to-warm-up babies aren't as intensely negative as difficult babies. They don't like new things, but they whimper rather than screaming, and they frown at new foods rather than recoiling violently and spewing those new foods back into the face of the person wielding the spoon. They're neither very happy nor very unhappy at any given time. But like difficult children, they do tend to learn to like new things eventually, although it takes them much longer to do so than it does easy babies.

Easy babies might be considered the "norm" of human temperament, in that they make up the largest temperament group explored by Thomas and Chess. About 40% of the babies they examined babies were classified as easy, versus 15% classified as slow-to-warm-up and only 10% classified as difficult. One could even argue that difficult babies were "abnormal," especially given how demanding their care is and how tired and miserable they make their parents.

But Thomas and Chess point out that it's not as simple as one kind of baby being easier to care for than another. They argue that the fit of the baby's temperament to his or her environment is key here. This is known as the **goodness of fit model.** The argument is a simple one—some temperaments are more suited for some environments, and others are more suited to other environments. The placid, cheerful easy babies thrive in environments where they're surrounded by attentive caretakers who feed them, clean them up, and respond to their discomforts even before the babies register them. But they wouldn't do as well with distracted, inattentive, busy, or overwhelmed caretakers. Their cheerful acceptance of discomforts might mean that they get less care in such situations.

By contrast, difficult babies may run the risk of driving their parents crazy. This may work to their disadvantage if they have impatient, hot-headed, intolerant parents. In extreme cases, difficult babies may be more at risk for infant battering or even of abandonment. Yet they also would provoke more attentive care from most parents. They won't sit placidly in soiled diapers developing major-league diaper rash because their parents are too busy to care for them. They won't be fed less than a twin brother or sister because they fuss less. Instead, they'll scream bloody murder until their parents tend to them, and only to them. The difficulty of caring for these children might also discourage their parents from having more children for a time, which may also work for the benefit of difficult babies as well.

Slow-to-warm-up babies also might inspire more caretaking in some situations than easy babies, urging caring but overwhelmed parents to work harder than those with easy babies to satisfy their children's needs. At the same time, such babies would be less at risk to battering or abandonment by impatient or frustrated parents than difficult babies.

Which type of baby is it best to be? As Chess and Thomas point out, it all depends on the parenting situation the child is going to have to deal with. It isn't a matter of the child's temperament, it's a matter of the fit of that temperament to the child's environment, including the temperaments and personalities of the parents. Each temperament pattern is advantageous in some situations, less advantageous in others, and disadvantageous in still others. The easy temperament is probably the one that is most advantageous most of the time, if its frequency of appearance in the population is any indication, and the difficult and slow-to-warm-up temperaments are probably more limited in the situations where they provide advantages for infants. But there must be situations where the latter two temperaments are advantageous, or they would have mostly bred out of the population generations ago.

In fact, geneticists note that, if almost everyone has one genetic tendency, it is often advantageous to have a genetic tendency that goes in another direction entirely. Most humans tend toward monogamy, for example, sticking with one sex partner for very long periods of time. This monogamy creates stable societies in which both mothers and fathers of children know whose children are their own, and thus both parents have an interest in making those children survive. In addition, monogamy means that we also know who our grandchildren are, and who our nieces and nephews are, and we can help make sure those children survive as well. Yes, "love-em and leave-em" type fathers might have a greater potential for spreading their genes far and wide, but their resulting children would have fewer caretakers ensuring their survival, and thus their greater number of children might not be as likely to survive and pass on the parents' genes.

Yet if most of the adult population is monogamous, then that creates a lovely wide-open niche for a few people to take advantage of the rest of us by sneaking around under the sheets attempting to impregnate people other than their monogamous partners. The resulting children might very well survive just fine, especially if the mother's unsuspecting monogamous partner doesn't know of the betrayal and raises the child as his own. As long as there aren't too many of these people scattering their seed far and wide, being different from the rest of the population can work out to a genetic advantage for them.

Of course, this difference is only going to be an advantage as long as there aren't too many people who have it. If more than a small fraction of the population sleeps around wantonly, fathers would start doubting the paternity of all their children, and those children of interlopers would have a much lower chance of survival.

Difficult children are in much the same situation. Most babies are either easy or slow-to-warm-up. Thus, most are less intense, less negative, and much, much less loud. A difficult baby might very well attract more than his or her share of parental attention and resources, especially if surrounded by easy babies who are less demanding. In a pair of twins or among siblings close in age, the difficult baby might be tended first and more often just because he or she demands it. The difficult baby might also be the first to respond to a new thing in the environment, such as an approaching snake or a possibly dangerous stranger, and respond loudly and energetic enough to demand immediate parental attention and rescue.

Ultimately, parents might like their easy babies better, might appreciate them more, enjoy spending time with them more, and have fonder memories of raising them. But difficult babies might have a mild survival edge even so, their very difference from their placid, happy siblings and cousins enabling them to grab more than their share of resources and care, if for no other reason than just to shut them up.

Reactivity, inclination toward sensation-seeking, susceptibility to drug use: these are just a few of the many genetic influences on human beings, influences that ensure that we aren't all created equal. To this list of qualities with a substantial genetic influence we could add various personality traits, including tendency toward extraversion, neuroticism, and conscientiousness, as well as various forms of intelligence, sheer physical bodily control, and a multitude of physical abilities.

This is one of the reasons that many psychologists argue that parents take far more credit for how their children turn out than they should. Some folks are blessed with cheerful, easy, nonreactive babies, babies who become adolescents with neurotransmitter balances that make drugs far less attractive to them and make participation in dangerous practices unpleasant. It's a lot easier to raise such children into productive adults with little in the way of misadventure than it is to do the same to children with difficult temperaments, children who find drugs highly pleasurable, and those who seek dangerous activities for the thrills associated with those activities. Parents generally follow what's known as the *self-serving bias* in these situations. We take credit for good outcomes, and we blame bad outcomes on factors other than ourselves. So when children turn out well, parents generally beam with pride and induce joint strain patting themselves on their backs, and when children turn out less well, we blame the environment outside the household and the children's innate tendencies. In truth, we'll never known how much of our success or failure in raising our children is due to just which sperm cell joined which egg cell, and thus what set of genes our children ended up with.

References:

Buckley, K. W. (1989). *Mechanical man: John broadus watson and the beginnings of behaviorism.* New York: Guilford.

Burroughs, E. R. (2008). *Tarzan of the apes.* New York: Signet Classics.

Chess, S., & Thomas, A. (1984). *Origins and evolution of behavior disorders: Infancy to early adult life.* New York: Burnner/Mazel.

Hobbes, T. (1997). *Leviathan: Authoritative text, backgrounds, interpre*tations (Richard E. Flathman & David Johnston, Eds.) New York: Norton.

Golding, W. (1999). *The lord of the flies.* London: Faber & Faber.

James, W. (1890) *The Principles of Psychology.* Retreived from http://psychclassics.yorku.ca/James/Principles/.

Kagan, J., & Fox, N. A. (2006). Biology, culture, and temperamental biases. In N. Eisenberg (Ed.) *Handbook of child psychology: Vol 3. Social, emotional, and personality development (6th Ed.)* Hoboken, NJ: Wiley.

Locke, J. (1996). *An essay concerning human understanding.* Indianapolis: Hackett.

Rousseau, J. J. (1987). *The basic political writings.* Indianapolis: Hackett.

Schuckit, M. A. (1998) *Biological, psychological, and environmental predictors of the alcoholism risk: A longitudinal study*. Journal of Studies on Alcohol, *59*, 485-494.

Thomas, A., & Chess, S. (1977). *Temperament and development*. New York: Brunner/Mazel.

Watson, J. B. (1930). *Behaviorism (revised edition).* Chicago: University of Chicago Press.

Zuckerman, M. (1994). *Behavioral expressions and the biosocial bases of sensation seeking*. Cambridge: Cambridge University Press.

Chapter 4: Teaching Old Dogs New Tricks

I did not direct my life. I didn't design it. I never made decisions. Things always came up and made them for me. That's what life is. B. F. Skinner

You can catch more flies with honey than with vinegar. Ancient English Proverb of unknown origin

The real question is not whether machines think but whether men do. The mystery which surrounds a thinking machine already surrounds a thinking man. B. F. Skinner

How do we teach an old dog new tricks, or a new dog old tricks, for that matter? In what ways are the same principles in training dogs involved in getting our children to do household chores? Why is your secret ambition to making other people dance to your tune probably doomed from the outset? How can you build a functioning spaceship from commonly available household items? I'll be answering all but one of these questions in this chapter. We'll begin by looking at a book about an fictional ideal society written by a tall, thin man with red hair.

Operant Conditioning, and Skinner's Utopian Vision

Back in 1948, B. F. Skinner, probably the second most famous psychologist in the world at the time, wrote a book in which he described, in fictional terms, his idea of an improved human society. The book was titled *Walden Two,* a reference to Henry David Thoreau's book *Walden; or, Life in the Woods*. Thoreau had written about his experiences living by Walden Pond for two years, including his attempts to embrace a simpler, more fulfilling life. More than 100 years later, Skinner described in *Walden Two* a visit to a fictional community as seen through the eyes of his protagonist, a university professor by the name of Professor Burris. In the novel, Professor Burris is inspired to look up his old colleague T. E. Frazier by some former students who have heard about Frazier's attempt at a utopian community and want to find out more about it. The group soon ends up at the doors of Walden Two, where Frazier, as the architect of the community, shows the initially skeptical group around his creation.

Frazier argues that through the use of scientifically applied behavioral modification principles and a healthy emphasis on reinforcement, he and his 1000 fellow residents have developed a model community. Children are raised communally by experts and people who enjoy child care, and are reinforced for behaving well and for enjoying the small pleasures of life rather than pursuing the rampant materialism of the outside world. With the total lack of inequity in either personal possessions or recognition for accomplishment, jealousy is supposedly nonexistent. Because the lives the residents live are simple and they aren't having to work for the expensive things most people pursue such as houses, vehicles, and other personal possessions, individuals need to work only a few hours a day and can spend the remaining time in hobbies, study, or leisure. Expert behaviorists administer the commune, altering the reinforcements available for various behaviors as needed to deal with problems as they arise. For example, if no one wants to do windows, work credit would be increased for that activity, and if everyone is competing to have a chance to use the Handy Dandy Dust Bunny Fluffer under the beds, work credit for that activity would be reduced until demand for the activity matches the need.

When some members of the visiting party argue that this is blatant manipulation of people of a most immoral sort, Frazier responds that all humans are manipulated in a like fashion, but that those in the outside world aren't usually aware of it. He also notes that when people are manipulated in the real world, they are generally being manipulated for the benefit of others, whereas Walden Two residents are being manipulated for their own benefit.

Some of the members of the group are impressed, and decide almost immediately to join the smoothly operating community. Some, like Professor Burris himself, are harder to convince, and at least one, Augustine Castle, is repulsed by what he sees and renounces it. When Burris points out that Frazier himself appears to be a seriously flawed individual, Frazier merely responds that he is the architect of Walden Two, not a product of it, and thus did not benefit from the social engineering that makes its members function so well within it. As the creator of his utopia, he himself will always be an outsider, able to appreciate it but never as much a part of it as its human products, the children who grew up within it.

Many analysts of *Walden Two* agree that Professor Burris and T. E. Frazier are actually alter egos of B. (Burrhus) F. (Frederic) Skinner himself, so that *Walden Two* is an internal dialogue within Skinner, a sort of exposition of his thought processes as he worked out in his own mind just how one might design a better society through the principles of behaviorism. The impossible to impress Augustine Castle, in turn, represents the established opinion, the group of people who are automatically opposed to the new and the different no matter how much evidence supports it. (The name "Augustine" means "venerated," or "ancient and established," so

Augustine Castle is literally "the ancient, established castle." There's an interesting quality of castles that led fairly quickly to them becoming outdated—they're stuck in one position and can't move or change. That's pretty clearly how Skinner views Castle's position—he's stuck in a position of opposing the whole idea of using behaviorism to improve the human condition or any departure from the old ways, for that matter, because he himself cannot adjust to such new conditions.)

The primary messages in Walden Two were later echoed in Skinner's more scholarly publication on the uses of behaviorism in improving society, a 1971 book entitled *Beyond Freedom and Dignity.* In this later publication, Skinner argued that the widespread belief in the freedom and dignity of human beings was an illusion, fostered by the fact that we simply aren't aware of the many ways we are controlled and manipulated by others. He argued that we needed a new view of human beings, a view that went "beyond freedom and dignity."

Throughout both publications, Skinner argued repeatedly that humans relied too much on punishment and not enough on reinforcement when trying to control and manipulate the behavior of other living things, be they people or animals. In *Walden Two,* for example, there is much mention of reinforcing the members of the community, but little mention of punishment. When punishment is mentioned, it's mentioned in negative terms. Frazier points out early on that a group of sheep at the community remain in a particular location and don't stray because they were exposed initially to an electric fence, teaching them not to move past a particular pair of posts, an action that resulted in a painful electric shock. The sheep learned to avoid moving past those posts, and thus thereafter avoided the punishment of the shocks, allowing the wire to be removed thereafter without the sheep attempting to escape. But later in the book, Frazier and Professor

Burris encounter a situation where a sheep has somehow gotten on the other side of the line between the two posts, and the sheep dog is having difficulty driving it back to the appropriate place because it refuses to cross that space that was associated with previous punishment. Frazier comments that the fault was in using punishment to start with rather than a reinforcement procedure, and that they need to work on a better way of training the sheep in the future.

Walden Two itself was not a big seller back in 1948 when it first came out, but it had a resurgence in sales in the 1960's, when a number of people were embracing Skinner's anti-materialist message and more than a few communes tried to emulate the rather sketchy blueprint he had created in the book. *Beyond Freedom and Dignity* inspired much debate in psychology departments but did not substantially change the American view of human beings, and it certainly didn't change our way of life. Are we missing a great opportunity here? Could we be bypassing the chance to form a truly great society because we cling to the romance of ideas like freedom, justice, and the dignity of human beings, and to a mythical belief in free will?

To investigate this issue, let's take a look, first, at areas where Skinner's behaviorism actually is quite successful. Then we'll examine the limitations that make his Walden Two more of a pipe dream than a workable model. (The phrase "pipe dream" is a colorful metaphor of well-known origins. Opium was traditionally smoked, often using a long pipe to keep the heat of the burning opium away from the face. People who smoke opium are prone to contemplating things they'd dearly love to have happen, and, while in the grips of an opium haze, often see everything working out the way they'd like it to with no practical impediments at all. Hence, unrealistic imaginings are often likened to the types of scenarios opium smokers spin, or "pipe dreams.")

The author of this particular pipe dream, B. F. Skinner, did not set out, specifically, to be a famous American psychologist. His first ambition was to be a writer. After graduating from college, he happened to come into a modest bequest from a dead relative and he made a pact with himself—he would write for a year and see if he was selling material and making progress toward notoriety by that point, and if not, he would go back to school and pursue the study of psychology instead. Once settled in to pursue his new profession, however, he soon realized that he'd hardly lived life at all, and thus had little of interest to write about. At the end of that year, dissatisfied with the dearth of good writing ideas he was able to come up with as well as his lack of progress in selling his work, he enrolled in graduate school at Harvard, where he began experimenting with how people and animals learned voluntary behavior. (Bjork, 1997) (The process of classical conditioning, dealing with how involuntary behavior was learned, had already been thoroughly explored by both Russian physiologist Ivan Pavlov and American Behaviorist John. B. Watson).

At the time, the most popular view of the learning of voluntary behavior was described in the work of Edward Thorndike, who did his most influential research from the early 1900's through the 1930's. Thorndike argued that the consequences of a behavior in any given situation determined its strength in the future. If a behavior in a given stimulus situation was followed by a good outcome, or what psychologists like to call "reinforcement," it was strengthened, but if in a given situation a behavior was followed by a bad outcome, as in a punishment, it would be weakened (Thorndike, 1911/1970).

Suppose, for example, we put a rat in what is known as a "T-maze." A T-maze is a very simple device. It's just a walled enclosure shaped like the letter "T." You place a hungry rat at the base of the "T" and let him loose. Having nowhere else to go, and being very hungry, the rat runs from the base to the top of the "T," at which point he finally does has a choice. He can go left, or go right. So let's suppose you pick one of those two choices at random, and set up the maze so he'll be reinforced for making that choice. Let's say we pick the right side. If the rat goes to the right, he gets a yummy rat meal of bread soaked in milk, or Purina Rat Chow, depending on what you prefer to serve up. (Early 20th Century behaviorist John Watson once claimed that he preferred to reward rats with bread soaked in milk, because he was constantly starving in his graduate school days and could eat the rat's food if the rat made the wrong choice).

If the rat goes to the left, he finds no food and is simply returned to his cage still hungry. So turning right has a good outcome, and turning left a bad outcome. Thorndike argued that rats who turned right would be more likely to turn right again when put in the maze at a future point, because right-turning behavior had a good outcome. Rats who turned left, on the other hand, would be less likely to turn left in the future and thus more likely to turn right, because turning left had a bad outcome, in that the rat had to wait even longer before eating. So over several trials, the rat should quickly learn to go right and not left and do so more quickly and surely each time. That, it turns out, was exactly what happened. Thorndike called his description of the rat's behavior the *Law of Effect.*

Thorndike was not totally happy with his Law of Effect, though. Toward the end of his career, he pointed out that it was disturbingly asymmetrical (Thorndike, 1911/1970). Positive outcomes made the behavior significantly more likely, but negative outcomes had only a small, sometimes almost imperceptible effect on reducing the chances of the behavior. In fact, rats and pigeons sometimes did behaviors with bad outcomes over and over again despite the fact they were being punished for those behaviors, a most disturbing state of affairs if you're trying to explain the rat's or pigeon's behavior. Skinner greatly simplified Thorndike's Law of Effect, resulting in what became known as *operant conditioning.* Dispensing with the whole discussion of good and bad outcomes, Skinner merely stated that behavior that is reinforced is more likely to occur again.

One thing you'll note immediately is that Skinner's operant conditioning, unlike Thorndike's Law of Effect, does not specifically note what happens when behaviors have bad outcomes, or, in other words, are punished. That's because punishments are unpredictable in outcome, as Thorndike himself had found out. (You can find discussion of the many and unpredictable effects of punishment in Chapter 3 of the companion volume of this series, *Psychology in Plain English.*) In general, if behavior that is reinforced becomes more common, then behavior that is punished will have to become less common, if only because there are only so many hours in the day, and if you're doing more of one behavior that leaves less time for another. But in the absence of a new behavior being reinforced, punished behaviors would probably continue to occur because the organism, whether it is a rat or a person, in many cases simply can't think of anything else to do, and thus has no other behavioral choices. By mentioning only reinforcement in describing operant conditioning, Skinner signaled that punishments play only a small role in the determination of behavior, a role usually strongly overshadowed by the effects of reinforcement.

The first thing to note about reinforcement is that it comes in two forms. *Positive reinforcers* are things that cause pleasure when they are brought to an organism, and thus the act of positive reinforcement involves the bringing of good things to an organism. Examples of positive reinforcement are giving people praise, strongly desired material goods, or, my personal favorite, high quality chocolate. The other type of reinforcers are *negative reinforcers*. Negative is the opposite of positive, so many people, including some psychologists, simply assume that negative reinforcement is the negative of reinforcement, or punishment. I can't tell you how may papers I've read in which a student has said, "I'd use a negative reinforcement, like taking away the child's video games." Taking away a valued thing isn't any form of reinforcement at all—it's punishment, quite the opposite of reinforcement. In this case, "positive" doesn't mean "good" in the term "positive reinforcement," and "negative" doesn't mean "bad" in the term "negative reinforcement." The terms refer to the presence and absence of the stimulus acting as a reinforcer in this case. Positive reinforcers are things that cause pleasure when brought or made present, and negative reinforcers are things that cause pleasure when taken away or made absent. Examples of negative reinforcement include removal of pain, removal of anxiety, or removal of hunger.

Let's say that 8-year-old Lutwidge has been told by his parents not to eat the berries on the tree outside her house. But he's sitting under the tree one day, he's hungry, the berries look good, and after awhile he gives in and eats several of them. Then he suddenly starts wondering if they're poisonous, and that's why he shouldn't eat them. He contemplates his stomach, and decides he is starting to feel a little funny. So Lutwidge runs into the house in panic. "Mommy, Mommy! I ate some of the berries on the tree outside! Am I going to die?"

After a quick chuckle, his mother explains that no, he's not going to die. The berries are just mulberries, and they had told Lutwidge not to eat them because they tended to get wormy and they didn't think he would want to eat them in that condition. Eight-year-old Lutwidge is immediately relieved. He's not going to die! He also just got negatively reinforced for taking problems to his mother—he took his worry to her mother, and his mother removed his anxiety. He's been reinforced for going to his mother, negatively reinforced, and he'll be more likely to go to her mother in the future.

It's actually fairly easy to remember. Bringing good things to an organism, including human beings, is positive reinforcement. Taking bad things away from an organism is negative reinforcement. Is there a similar distinction for forms of punishment? Yes, there is. Bringing bad things to an organism is positive punishment, and taking away good things is negative punishment. Reinforcers are always good, punishments are always bad. Taking away a child's video game is a bad thing, so it's punishment. Taking way his anxiety is a good thing, so it's a reinforcement.

Some actions can be both positively and negatively reinforcing. Food, for example, is pleasurable to taste, chew, and swallow, making it a positive reinforcer, and also removes hunger, making it a negative reinforcer. Foods such as cotton candy, which taste good but aren't very filling, are primarily positive reinforcers. Foods such as those plain rice cakes (you know, the things that look like little disks of Styrofoam, and taste, well, like little disks of Styrofoam), boiled turnips, or my daughter's favorite example, kale, are primarily negative reinforcers—they aren't a lot of fun to eat, but they do stave off hunger.

Skinner's entire career was spent primarily on studying the effects of different types and schedules of reinforcement on the subsequent behavior of animals. One of his biggest targets was what are called "reinforcement contingencies," which refers to just what triggers the reinforcement (such as passage of time or number of responses) and how frequently the reinforcement is triggered (such as every response, every 10 minutes, or about every 100th response). Let's say, for example, that you want your child to empty the trash in the household trashcans into the big city trashcan on a regular basis (and who doesn't—the alternative is having to do it yourself). You decide to reinforce the behavior of taking out the trash so that it will occur in a frequent and timely fashion. Your first impulse might be to use what is called *continuous reinforcement.* You vow to give the child a sum of money for every time a household trash can is taken outside and dumped in the big bin. That would probably work (provided the child likes money and you're offering enough to get his or her attention), and the trash would probably get emptied regularly. But it also means that you'd be passing out money really, really frequently. You couldn't, therefore, make the amount of money very big, or pretty shortly you'd be dipping into the child's college fund. Yet if you make the amount small, offering him, for example, ten cents for every can he empties, the reward may be so close to nothing that the child will probably start thinking that there's not much point in this trash disposal gig. So you come up with a brilliant idea. You tape a sheet of paper on the wall in some unobtrusive place, and you tell the child to check off a box on the paper every time he takes out a trash can. Once he's checked off ten boxes, you promise him to reinforce him with a whole dollar. Now note that we're still rewarding him at the same level—we've just changed *when* we're giving the reinforcements—a dollar for 10 behaviors rather than a tenth that for one behavior. But your child is pretty young, and a dollar is a sizeable sum of money, money that you can actually buy something with. And all he has to do to earn that sum of money is to take the trash out ten times.

What we're using here by giving the child a reinforcement every so many times he does a behavior is what Skinner called *fixed ratio reinforcement.* We're reinforcing the child for every time he does a fixed number of responses. Fixed ratio reinforcement has a number of interesting qualities. For one thing, it results in pretty steady responding, and fairly frequent responding as well, because the more frequently your child takes out trash cans in a given time period, the more money he'll make. There is a tendency for both people and animals on fixed ratio reinforcement to take a breather just after each reward, because they know it'll be awhile before they get the next one. But those breaks don't tend to be long, because the sooner you get started, the sooner you get the next reward. Fixed ratio reinforcement is used by many employers—it's especially useful in situations where you want employees to work as steadily and rapidly as possible, to maximize their total output.

Now, let's do something a little different, just to shake things up a bit. We tell our child that, instead of rewarding him every tenth time he takes out the trash, we'll reward him every tenth time, more or less. That is, we'll average a dollar reward every tenth time he takes out the trash, but on an unpredictable schedule. So he might get rewarded the tenth time he takes out the trash, or the eighth, or the twelfth, or the twentieth. He might even get rewarded twice in a row. Such a reward schedule is called *variable ratio reinforcement.* You're still going to get rewarded, you just no longer know exactly which response is going to trigger the reward. So put yourself in the child's place—how is this new reward schedule going to change your responding?

One thing hasn't changed—you still get more rewards the more frequently you do the behavior during any particular span of time. So the incentive to get right at the task is still there. What has changed is the predictability of the reward itself. Any given response might be the one that is rewarded. So how hard are you going to work? And how long are you going to keep at it? If you're like the average person, rat, or pigeon, you'll work steadily and rapidly, maybe even more rapidly than you did for fixed ratio reinforcement. For one thing, there's no reason to take a breather after each reinforcement is earned, because you might still be rewarded for the very next response. At the same time, if it's been awhile since you were last reinforced, you also could be reinforced for the very next response. In fact, the longer the string of responses that you give without a reward, the more you'll probably be sure that the reinforcement is coming any second! You'll also tend to work longer before quitting, because there's no good stopping point like there is with fixed ratio reinforcement. With fixed ratio reinforcement, the natural place to stop is just after receiving a reinforcement. After all, the next reinforcement is now guaranteed to be some number of responses into the future. But with variable ratio reinforcement this isn't the case, so after a reinforcement, you might as well get right back to work.

If offered such a pay scale, many wouldn't opt for variable ratio reinforcement because they don't like the unpredictability of it. We want to know just when we're going to be paid, and how much. Yet other people would pick it for just that reason—they like the excitement of the unpredictability. And even for those who aren't paid in this way, variable ratio reinforcement plays a big, big role in our lives. Recognition by others, attention, and praise are, more or less, received on a variable ratio schedule. Folks notice the good behaviors we do now and then, but not after predictable, regular number of instances of those good behaviors. Yet those smiles of appreciation and those moments of public acknowledgment are apt to inspire dogged pursuit of the praised behavior for weeks to follow.

The other place where we constantly experience variable ratio reinforcement is when we deal with games of chance. Picture a person playing a slot machine. Slot machines are generally required by law to be variable ratio reinforcement devices. That is, each time you put your money or tokens in and pull the lever, the machine is supposed to have a particular probability of paying off a jackpot. Thus, you'll get rewarded for every so many plays on the average, but those payoffs will not occur regularly or predictably. That's actually what makes the machine most compelling. The most important quality of variable ratio reinforcement is there in spades – the very next time you pull the lever, the machine might possibly pay off. That's true whether it's just paid a jackpot, or whether it hasn't paid over many, many pulls. And that potential for the very next pull to be the big payoff is what keeps the inveterate gambler going. Even the big losers.

That may be the most intriguing quality of variable ratio reinforcement—it has a powerful resistance to extinction. Extinction is what often happens if we stop the reinforcement for a particular behavior. After some time, when the behavior is clearly no longer gaining reinforcement, most organisms, including both people and animals, gradually reduce doing the behavior and then stop it completely. The behavior is then replaced by other behaviors that are being reinforced instead.

Consider the case of fixed ratio reinforcement above. We've been reinforcing our nine-year-old for every ten times he takes out the trash on a regular basis. What happens if we stop reinforcing him? He probably will keep up the behavior initially, when we skip the first reinforcement, guessing that the reinforcement is just delayed and will come soon. He may even continue through the twentieth or even thirtieth response, when the second and third reinforcement would have been expected. But then he'll probably give up, stop taking out the trash, and the behavior will have undergone extinction.

Now consider the same child being reinforced using variable ratio reinforcement. Unlike the example above, this child isn't getting reinforced predictably, and thus if we stop the reinforcement, at first he probably isn't even going to notice that he's no longer being reinforced. After all, he's gone twenty or even thirty responses in the past between reinforcements, this being balanced by the times reinforcement has come successively or almost successively. So the longer he goes without reinforcement, the more sure he becomes that reinforcement is just around the corner, and that he doesn't dare stop now for fear that he'll miss out on it when it comes if he stops. Thus, variable ratio reinforcement is incredibly resistant to extinction, quite notoriously so. One of my professors from my undergraduate days once related this example. They were doing an experiment with a rat where the rat was on a variable ratio schedule with a very large number of responses required for each reinforcement, in the neighborhood of hundreds of bar presses for each rat pellet. They left the experiment running overnight, with an automatic hopper to provide the pellets each time they were earned. The hopper holding the food became blocked, however, soon after they left. This meant that after a short while the reinforcements stopped for the bar pressing, because the flow of food from it was blocked. When the experimenters returned at eight the next morning, they found an exhausted rat still doggedly pressing the bar, working for its next reinforcement despite having not been reinforced for hours. (We always claim when we feel overworked that we've been "working like a dog" or "working doggedly." Maybe we should say we've been "working like a rat" or "working rattedly. " Just a thought.)

So behaviors driven by variable ratio reinforcements are incredibly resistant to extinction. This is one of the reasons why gambling is so very, very addictive. People gamble for a variety of reasons—because they enjoy the thrill and anticipation of the win, because they like the excitement of the chase, because they dream of being wealthy, or because they believe they'll solve all of their problems with one big win. All of these are reinforcers, but they're all predicated on winning. Losing very often is actually a form of extinction, because you're doing the behavior over and over again and not getting the reinforcer. It can even be a form of punishment if you view it in terms of your valuable money, something you like, being taken away.

There are also some gambling situations where skill plays a role, and thus losing is not guaranteed. Some people actually are reliably reinforced for gambling. Poker, for example, involves a little bit of skill in, as Kenny Rogers pointed out, knowing when to hold them, when to fold them, what to throw away, and what to keep. Even more skill is involved in poker in reading the "tells" of others, manipulating your own tells and expressions, and bluffing convincingly. If you're good enough, poker isn't quite so much a game of chance. Betting on sports events also involves skill to some degree.

The favorites of the casinos, though, are the games governed mostly or completely by chance. Blackjack requires mild amounts of skill, in knowing when the odds favor staying or hitting, splitting or doubling down. But these only mildly affect the outcomes. The big factors in winning at poker, such as tells and bluffing, play no role in blackjack. The dealer's behavior in hitting or staying on his or her own hand is completely mechanical, governed by rules, and the dealer wouldn't behave any differently if he or she knew what cards you held. On the average, you'll lose playing blackjack, because the rules are such that the odds favor the house, if only ever so slightly. Most other betting games are completely governed by chance, such as roulette and the slot machines. Because of the zero (and possibly double zero) on the roulette wheel, and because the odds of the slots are set to favor the house, one is more likely to lose than to win playing those games. So what keeps gamblers playing day and night, even when they haven't won in many pulls of the handle or drops of the ball?

Consider this bit of irony--a prominent former US cabinet member once wrote a very well-received book on the need for self-control and self-discipline in individuals. He then reportedly lost almost all of the millions of dollars in royalties from the book in high-stakes gambling. Losing that much money would have to involve some horrendous losing streaks. So why didn't this individual stop gambling after those horrendous losses? Why, once he'd lost a million or two, didn't the now unreinforced behavior extinguish? That's the thing with variable ratio reinforcement. Even when you haven't been reinforced in many, many responses, you don't want to quit. You just keep plugging away, waiting for that next reinforcement that you're sure is coming. Ironically, the longer you go without reinforcement, the more sure you become that it's just around the corner, and the more avidly you continue gambling! The gambler is compelled to play whether winning or losing. While winning, he or she is being reinforced for playing, and when losing, he or she simply becomes more and more certain that a winning streak is "due."

This feeling that a win is due is an important part of what is known as "the gambler's fallacy." The gambler's fallacy is the belief that past random events have some influence on what is going to happen next. This includes the common belief in "winning streaks," and "losing streaks," and the common gambler's belief that if you've lost many times in a row, you're "due." It's a great recipe for losing vast quantities of cash. The gambler's fallacy helps keep people playing even when they're losing heavily, because they believe that past random events influence upcoming ones, so that they're "due" to win.

Another situation where problems arise from variable ratio reinforcement pops up all the time in the grade school classroom. In Chapter 3 of the first volume of this series, *The Punishment Myth,* we talked about attention pigs, the children in the classroom who are bored easily and often disrupt class for the sheer excitement and stimulation of it. What I didn't mention in that chapter is that these classroom disruptions are usually being reinforced on a variable ratio reinforcement schedule. Mostly, the kid's behaviors, his or her frequent bids for attention, are ignored. Once in awhile, they might be punished (but not often—there just isn't that much a teacher can do to punish these outbursts). And once in a great while, the behavior actually gets reinforced—the kid has everyone in class laughing and approving, and even the teacher has to smile at his antics. It's a classic variable ratio reinforcement schedule, with large reinforcements popping up every so many disruptions, but not predictably.

Now let's say that the teacher in this situation has read about operant conditioning, and decides to extinguish this behavior by trying to make sure that the disruptive child doesn't ever get reinforced for his or her disruptions. So this teacher ignores the child's outbursts, or distracts the other children's attention each time the attention pig does one of his or her antics, thus robbing our attention pig of his or her reinforcement. The teacher's plan is to do this until the behaviors of the disruptive child extinguish, thus improving dramatically the classroom atmosphere.

It's really not a bad plan. But the problem is that we're dealing with variable ratio reinforcement, and it's very resistant to extinction. The child has gone many, many responses in the past between reinforcements, and they've always been unpredictable. As we engage in our extinction procedure, robbing him or her of each reinforcement that would otherwise have come, our attention pig probably will, for an extended period of time, simply try harder for that reinforcement that he or she is sure is coming any second, perhaps the very next time he does something disruptive. And if our intrepid teacher fails, even once, to deny the attention pig his or her reinforcement, the worst possible outcome will happen—

we'll have simply converted the reinforcement schedule to a variable ratio reinforcement with more responses between reinforcements. Sadly, that makes the behavior even harder to extinguish.

Skinner pointed out that both extinction and punishment were slow and ineffective in situations like this, extinction for the reasons cited above, and punishment because punishment is also a source of attention and probably will increase the disruptive behavior of our attention-seeking little swine. The solution to corralling the attention pigs? Reinforcing the behavior you want, so that it becomes more frequent, thus reducing the incidences of producing the behavior you don't want. Skinner would suggest we set up a contract with the disruptive child that gives him certain reinforcements or privileges for each period of time during which he fails to disrupt class. As he increases his rates of nondisruptive behavior in order to gain the reinforcement, disruptive behavior would decrease. Because reinforcement works more rapidly and controllably than can ever be accomplished by extinction, this improvement would come right away. And because reinforcement is pleasurable, it would not lead to a generalized dislike of school, a risk we'd run if we were to use punishment on the child.

In addition to fixed and variable ratio reinforcement, there are other sorts of reinforcement schedules. Some are based on the passage of time rather than on a specific number of responses. A fixed interval schedule, for example, involves the situation where reinforcement occurs after the passage of a period of time, such as so many minutes, hours, or days. Imagine, for example, that you're a hungry street person. There's a mission down the street that will provide street people with food twice a day, at 6 AM and 6 PM. Food is very reinforcing when you're hungry. So the act of going down the street to the mission is being reinforced. The problem is that you can't get that positive reinforcer when you choose—it won't come until we reach the proper time. At that point, the reinforcement becomes available for a time, then it won't be present again for another 12 hours. Thus, going to the mission is reinforced, but on a fixed interval schedule. Nothing you do can hasten when the next outcomes, but once it's due, it's available the very next time you walk down to the mission.

So what effect does this have on frequency of the behavior? My guess would be that you won't even consider going toward the mission at all until it's near the time for the next meal. Once that time gets close, though, you'll probably hike right over there with great dispatch. And once you've gotten your reinforcement, you won't go back to the mission until near the time the next reinforcement is due.

In truth, this is actually a more appropriate reinforcement schedule to use on our 9-year-old in the trash emptying situation than either fixed or variable-ratio reinforcement. Fixed interval reinforcement is ideal in situations where we simply want the behavior to occur on a regular basis, but not frequently and not necessarily rapidly—situations where we just want the job to get done. That's the case in our trash-emptying example—all we really want is that the trash go out the night before the cans have to be placed by the curb. We really don't need him emptying the cans in the house multiple times a day just to pad his reinforcement, and that's what he'd do in the case of either fixed or variable ratio reinforcements. So we tell our 9-year-old that we'll give him a dollar every week if the trash goes out by Tuesday night (trash day being Wednesday at our house). That means that taking out the trash on Friday, or Saturday, or even Monday isn't going to happen. But as the reinforcement gets near, the child will, eventually, unlimber the behavior and take the trash out. Then he'll grab his dollar, and he won't touch a can until next Tuesday. Still, that's sufficient for our needs, and ultimately will cost us less than paying him based on his rate of behavior.

Most of us aren't on fixed interval reinforcement schedules, either. Instead, most of us are reinforced on what's called *fixed duration reinforcement.* Fixed duration reinforcement involves reinforcing the organism for continuing a particular behavior across a time interval. Everyone paid by the hour, week, or month is on fixed duration reinforcement. As long as they're doing the behavior over the time period, they get paid. Say you're running a hoity-toity department store, with hoity-toity customers who wish to be waited on hand and foot. You wouldn't want to pay your employees on commission, which would be a form of fixed ratio reinforcement. If we did, they'd probably try to rush your customers, and push them to buy things that don't suit them in order to maximize their reinforcements. They're not going to stand for you paying them on a variable ratio schedule, either. Fixed interval reinforcement is totally inappropriate—your employees will only work when payday is near in that case. But fixed duration reinforcement is perfect. You're paying your people for engaging in serving the customers for as long as the customers are there, thus making your hoity-toity customers feel important. (I, personally, don't patronize hoity-toity department stores. I try very hard not to be hoity-toity. I am, I'll admit, sometimes hoity, and I've even been toity a time or two, but I try very hard not to be both at the same time).

You've probably noticed by now that there's no one proper reinforcement schedule. Different circumstances call for some types of reinforcement, and others call for another. And sometimes reinforcement occurs quite by accident. It's the results of that situation that we're going to look at next.

Supersitious Behavior

One of the most captivating contentions by Skinner was his proposal concerning the cause of superstitious behavior. Superstitious behavior describes situations where we believe we are causing a particular positive outcome by our behavior when in fact we are not. Skinner first observed superstitious behavior in pigeons when he decided to reinforce a hungry pigeon with food at closely spaced but random intervals, and see what happened. What happened was that the pigeons tended to increase the frequency of whatever they were doing when the reinforcement came. For example, if a pigeon happened to have just turned to the side and then the reinforcement pellet dropped, it would tend to turn to the side more often after that. That meant that when the next reinforcement came, it probably also landed at a time when the pigeon was turning to the side, and that increased the behavior even more. Before long, the pigeon would be whirling in continuous circles, stopping only to pick up the reinforcements that continued to arrive randomly. The pigeon was acting as if under the mistaken belief that its turning in circles was creating the reinforcement.

Skinner pointed out that the same process occurs in humans just as readily, and suggested this process was responsible for superstitious behavior. People receive reinforcement that occurs at random or due to some other cause, but mistakenly assume was due to something they did. They then repeat the behavior, and because they do, every now and then they get reinforced right after doing the behavior. That appears to the individual in much the same way variable ratio reinforcement appears. That is, the people appear to be being reinforced for the behavior regularly but unpredictably. So they react like someone being given variable ratio reinforcement—they increase the frequency of the behavior.

Now it would be reasonably easy for these people who've been randomly rewarded to demonstrate that their actions aren't causing the reinforcement—all they'd have to do is to stop the superstitious behavior entirely for a time and wait, and they'd soon see that the reinforcements continued even when the behavior stopped. But they're unlikely to do that, mainly because they're afraid to run the risk of losing the reinforcement they've been getting all along that they've been mistakenly attributing to their behavior.

There are other reasons they're unlikely to challenge their belief that they're controlling the reinforcements as well. To do so would be to admit that they have no control over the outcome at all, and that's anxiety-creating for most humans (more about controllability and the anxiety caused by uncontrollability can be found in Chapter 6: *Accentuating the Positive*). Also, it's likely that the person doesn't have any other behavior queued up, just waiting to jump in and replace the original superstitious behavior. Stopping the superstitious behavior would simply leave a behavioral vacuum in that case. Also, the behavior has probably become comforting and pleasurable, because we've paired it with positive outcomes in our mind. Also, humans simply have a hard time judging the frequency of relatively rare events, and tend to see the results they want to see or expect to see. (This is an issue discussed in Chapter 1 of *Psychology in Plain English,* the first volume of this series). Thus, if the person were to stop the superstitious behavior, they might perceive the reinforcements as diminishing even if they really aren't, because they're expecting them to diminish. As a result of all these things, people engaging in superstitious behavior almost never realize they're not really causing the reinforcements, and so, once established, superstitious behavior is unlikely to be extinguished. (Isn't it marvelous the way all this stuff comes together?)

My wife and I have a dear old aunt of highly advanced age (we'll call her Myrtle) who loves to take the senior citizen buses to gambling centers, where she plays the slot machines, eats from the buffets, and periodically enjoys a nip from the flask she keeps in her purse, replenishing it as needed from the free drinks that she's offered while playing. Some time back she returned happy and excited at having won a reasonably large slot machine jackpot, a jackpot in the neighborhood of hundreds of dollars. (Public service message: winning a jackpot of hundreds of dollars is a rare occurrence when playing the slots, folks—don't consider this example evidence you ought to run off with the family fortune and convert it all into chips). As I was congratulating her on her good fortune (and carefully ignoring the topic of how many dollars she'd run behind in the many trips prior to that point), she triumphantly reported that she'd actually worked out how to make the machines pay off more frequently. "I know the secret," she said, looking up at me and beckoning me to lean over so that she could speak more softly, apparently not wanting this secret to get out. "It's all in how you pull the lever," she said to me, with a conspiratorial look. "You see, most people pull it too fast, and it doesn't pay off if you pull it that fast. You've got to start out slow, than pull it faster as it comes down. Start off slow, then gradually get faster. Then it pays off more."

"Aunt Myrtle," I said. "Slot machines these days are all electronic devices. They have a switch on the handle that registers when the handle has been pulled down, and it cues the random number generator inside. The random number generator spits out a random number, and that number is matched to a table in the machine's memory that tells what display it should bring up, and whether to pay off or not, and if so, how much. All the handle does is trigger it to come up with a number. I'm pretty sure it doesn't care how fast or slow you close the switch when you pull the lever."

She listened to me very patiently, nodding throughout my speech. "Just remember," she said when I stopped talking. "Don't pull the lever fast right away. Start out slow, then sneak up on it. It'll pay off more."

My guess is that she'll pull slot machine levers that way the rest of her life, which I'm hoping will be quite a long time, yet. She believes she's affecting the outcome, she feels better believing that, and she's not likely to ever test her belief by changing the way she pulls the lever, because she fears that would reduce her payoffs. And even if she did conduct such an experiment, the nature of variable ratio reinforcement is such that she might have a hard time judging if the payoffs had changed as a result of her test, anyway.

So that's the long and the short of operant conditioning and how it affects us. What does all of this to do with Skinner's *Walden Two?* One of Skinner's main points throughout the novel is that if we designed the environment right, humans could be reinforced to do things that were good for them and the community. Because they were being reinforced for doing these things, people would be happy and content. They'd experience little anxiety, they'd associate most of their surroundings and activities in their lives with good feelings, and they'd interact with others in positive ways because that's what they'd been reinforced to do. Skinner didn't pretend that he knew exactly how his Walden Two should be constructed in detail. It's clear that he assumed that this would have to be done by the managers of the community, social scientists who would constantly analyze situations in the community and change reinforcements and environments on the fly as needed to deal with whatever problems came up. The environment would be set up to reinforce positive, necessary behaviors, and people would react to those reinforcements by adjusting their behaviors. Skinner doesn't argue that such a life is for everyone. In the guise of Frazier, Walden Two community guide and Skinner alter-ego, he admits that there would be people who really don't fit into such a community. In the book, Frazier in fact tells his guests that such misfits are encouraged to depart the community and find an environment in the outside world that suits them more completely. But he also suggests that such people aren't common, and that most who don't fit have problems because they haven't been raised in the Walden Two community and thus haven't benefited from the conditioning that children of that community.

Could we create Heaven on Earth through operant conditioning, as Skinner proposed so many years ago? It's hard to say. People have, at various times since the publication of his book, tried to form communities loosely similar to what he describes, but most differed from what he proposed in fundamental ways and thus were not true tests of his proposal, and many failed for reasons having nothing to do with the principles of behaviorism. Still, critics have argued that Skinner's vision is too mechanistic, too manipulative, or too simplistic to actually succeed. Humans are affected by operant conditioning, these people argue, but those effects aren't as simple as Skinner suggested. One such caution comes from the work of Albert Bandura.

Bandura is famous for his studies of imitation in humans. Way back in the 1960's, Bandura, like many people, became concerned that movies and television were exposing children to lots and lots of violent behavior, and wondered if that violent behavior was influencing children negatively (Bandura, 1973). In a series of landmark studies, he showed boys, one at a time, a film of a child entering a room full of toys, then approaching a blow-up clown doll and proceeding to beat it up in a number of distinctive ways while saying distinctive things. After seeing the film, the children were taken to the very room full of toys that appeared in the film and told they could play there for a time. They were left alone, but their actions were recorded. A significant number of children imitated the boy in the film, beating up the blow-up clown and uttering the same distinctive things while doing so.

In later studies, Bandura found, not surprisingly, that children are more likely to imitate the filmed models if the models were reinforced after beating up the clown doll rather than punished. But a third condition in this latter series of studies did provide some intriguing results—Bandura found that children were just as likely to imitate the model's attacks on the clown doll when the model's actions were ignored as when they were reinforced. Later studies, as well as real world events, have verified this result—when behavior that would normally be punished is being ignored, that inspires as much imitation as if the behavior was being reinforced. So if normally no one is allowed to walk on the lawn in the quad at your child's middle school, but today some students venture onto it and the teachers ignore them, before long the lawn will be covered with students. Likewise, in city after city when there have been blackouts and a few people have started looting, police have discovered that immediate response is important—if looting is occurring and police don't appear to be responding, even more people begin looting, and the effect can explode quickly out of control, as it did during the Los Angeles riots of 1992.

Many people have argued that the Bandura studies provide strong evidence that children imitate the aggressive actions they see on TV and movies, but that's debatable. After all, the children in the study, and the boy in the film, aren't really engaging in aggression at all—they're beating up a doll, a doll that was actually designed, originally, as a punching target for children. In addition, the whole experiment can't help but suggest to the participant children that they should imitate the actor in the film—they're shown a film of his actions with no accompanying commentary, then they're taken right to where the child did those actions. What else could the experimenter be expecting the child to do but imitate the model? It's possible that we're just seeing is called reactivity, where participants in an experiment act in certain ways because they believe that's what they're supposed to do (Reactivity is discussed in Chapter 1 of the first volume of this series, *The Science of Psychology*).

But whether it demonstrates that children imitate aggressive actions from TV or not, Bandura's overall work on imitation points out just how important it is as a learning mechanism in humans, and how much we learn just by observing other people and then doing what they do. Sure, operant conditioning plays a role in human behavior, but so does observational learning, and the latter's role is probably much more significant that operant conditioning for most of us. Unlike rats and pigeons, we don't have to be reinforced for a behavior in order to do it—we'll do it if we see other humans reinforced for it. It's intriguing, when you read *Walden Two*, how Skinner doesn't really mention using observational learning, role models, and imitation in influencing the behavior of his community residents and in rearing the children, even though such influences are normally powerful ones in the real world. In fact, at one point community leader Frazier denies that he's leading a cult of personality or that his feelings toward Walden Two influence other community members at all, as if people don't routinely imitate their leaders, especially beloved leaders with prestige and power.

Bandura is also responsible for another important principle of human behavior that would make the *Walden Two* community problematic to actually implement. This principle goes by the impressive name of *reciprocal control* or *reciprocal determinism* (Bandura, 1997). Reciprocal control is actually a fairly simple idea. The general premise is that in any reinforcement situation, reinforcement is a two-way street, in that while Person A is influencing Person B by reinforcing him or her, Person B is doing the same thing back to Person A. It's not the sort of thing that Skinner was likely to notice in his own research, because he was experimenting mostly with rats and pigeons. When you put a pigeon in a box and reinforce it with a food pellet every time it does a particular behavior, it's pretty clear you're the one manipulating the pigeon, because you set up that environment, the pigeon really can't do anything to alter it, and you control the reinforcement contingencies. But in real world situations using humans, we don't have sole control of the environment, and the person we're reinforcing *is reinforcing us back in return.*

Let's say that you want little Lutwidge to do better in spelling. Spelling ability is more a matter of practice than anything else. Pretty much anyone can learn to spell any word if they practice long enough and hard enough (although as we've already discussed, in English, spelling is a bit harder than in some other language, and might take more practice). So you tell Lutwidge that you want him to practice his spelling list at least 15 minutes a day Monday through Thursday, and to get 100% on his spelling test on Friday. If he does, you promise to reinforce him by taking him to the park for 2 hours on Saturday morning and playing ball with him there, an activity he dearly loves. You're the adult, you're giving the reinforcements, you're setting up the reinforcement contingencies, so you're clearly controlling Lutwidge, right?

Hah! You say. I know a set-up question when I hear one--you do one in just about every chapter. Well, you're right—this is a set-up question. Because so far we've only looked at this from your point of view as the parent. Now let's look at it from Lutwidge's point of view. In this case, the behavior he wants to increase in you is taking-to-the-park behavior. So what he's doing is reinforcing you with what you want, the studying of spelling and higher spelling grades, so that you'll increase your taking-to-the-park behavior.

Who's actually controlling whom? That's hard to say. We'll truly know only if the contingencies slide a bit (something reinforcement contingencies often do). Suppose that you have a very tiring week on the road selling Handy Dandy Dust Bunny Fluffers, even though each one comes, as everyone knows, with the dryer lint attachment, smokeless astray, and a knife strong enough to cut through a tin can and still slice a tomato. You explain to Lutwidge that you simply can't get up early enough Saturday morning to take him to the park, but you'll resume your agreement in the following week. If Lutwidge continues to study just as hard the next week and to get good spelling grades, clearly you were controlling him, and you can probably miss a Saturday now and then in the future and he'll still keep studying. But let's say that it's Lutwidge who has a bad week. He doesn't study one of the days, and then he misses one of the spelling words on Friday as well. But he looks at you with his puppy-dog eyes and says, "Can't we go to the park anyway? The only reason I didn't study on Tuesday was because I had to take out the garbage, and it was a lot for only a dollar! And besides, the word I missed was antidisestablishmentarianism, and I don't even know what that means!" If you then take pity on him and take him to the park anyway (and who wouldn't—what kind of spelling word is that, and when is he ever going to use it, anyway, if he does learn to spell it?), then clearly Lutwidge is controlling you.

The bottom line is that in human situations like this, reinforcement always goes two directions, and who's in control depends on who cares the most. Before they have children, parents often view themselves as being the puppet masters who will manipulate their children into being whatever they envision for the child. They're like early behaviorist John B. Watson, believing that they can form any child into anything they want given the right environment and enough time (Watson, 1930).

But Bandura's reciprocal control suggests a different view. In his model, the puppet master can pull, but the puppet pulls back, and sometimes the puppet pulls back more strongly than the puppet master cares to. When that happens, the puppet itself is in control. This is a phenomenon most parents experience as their children grow. They start out with big plans for their children's lives and activities, and often end up somewhere else entirely, a place that's the product of the joint pull between them and their child (and the myriad other environmental forces acting upon the child). Reciprocal control would also make Skinner's *Walden Two* much more difficult than Skinner suggests. The managers could certainly try to set reinforcers and environmental contingencies, but the residents would immediately start trying to distort those reinforcers and contingencies in order to maximize their own reinforcements. The managers would have more power, but the residents would outnumber them. It's impossible to tell how it would all end up when the dust settled, but I'd put my money on the residents.

That doesn't mean that a greater use of operant conditioning in our everyday affairs, our business dealings, our child rearing, and our relations with others wouldn't be a good idea. People often forget that humans respond more readily to reinforcement than to punishment. One place I saw this need over and over occurred during the years my children were in youth sports. My personal view is that youth sports are generally a good thing—children clearly need exercise and benefit from learning skills in controlling their bodies, they get a lot of self-satisfaction and pride from sports activities, and the whole family benefits from getting out of the house and into the outside air once in awhile. Many of the children in youth sports, especially the youngest children, enjoy youth sports just for the chance to run and jump and participate, whether they're good at them, mediocre, or absolutely atrocious. But this sheer exuberance is often squelched over the years by youth sports coaches. Youth sports coaches are generally volunteers from the pool of parents whose children are in those youth sports. They're a diverse group of people. Some are simply parents who stepped up because no one else was volunteering. Some are people who believe in the ideals of the sports organization and want to embody them and teach them to the children. Some just welcome the chance to share experiences with their children. But most are avid players of the sport themselves—people who've gone through the sports at all levels from the kindergarten years onward, until age or lack of ability or the need to pursue a living limited their continued participation.

The people in this latter group tend to have two things in common: The sport, and being good at it, is very, very important to them, and their most recent exposure to the sport as participants has been at an advanced level, such as high school or college competition, where winning was everything and total dedication and grueling practice was the norm. People at the advanced levels of sports are often already strongly motivated to do well. A coach who barks at these advanced athletes, who criticizes, mocks, and threatens punishments may provide that little extra incentive that gets the most out of them. At these levels, too, the goal is to win, so getting the most out of the players to obtain that win becomes the paramount thing, not the well-being of the players.

But youth sports, especially early youth sports, isn't just a different kettle of fish, it's on a different stove in a different kitchen in another country. Let's face it—who wins the local Little League or Pony League Championship just doesn't matter, not in the grand scheme of things. There was a different champion last year, there will be a different champion next year, and nobody will remember if your child's team won or lost. Heck, most people can't even remember who won an event as momentous as the Little League World Series just a few weeks after it happens, let alone a few years later. The little kids, especially, don't care that much—they win, they lose, either way they go back to school and on with life.

The thing relevant to our discussion that I've observed about many youth sports coaches over the years is their extraordinary tendency to rely on punishment as their major way of dealing with and getting the most out of the children under their care. The kids don't seem to be paying attention? Have them run laps, or do pushups. A kid drops the ball, or makes the wrong play? Yell, and threaten to take the kid out of the lineup. Kids grumble about the length of the practice? Make the practice even longer, and tell them that you'll make it longer yet if they keep grumbling.

Yet as Skinner pointed out, punishments are not nearly as effective as reinforcement in motivating behavior, nor nearly as direct in doing so. Rather than punishing the child who isn't paying attention, he'd suggest praising the child who is. Instead of yelling at the kid who drops the ball, he'd advocate we ignore that and praise him when he makes the play during a later attempt. In lieu of punishing children when they grumble, Skinner would argue that we should reinforce children who put in the extra effort and stay longer. Not only will children work their butts off for a little praise and recognition, but they'll also generalize those good feelings from being praised to participating in the sport itself and to the coaches who praise them, strengthening the love of playing and the coach-player bond.

When coaches use punishment, the bad feelings raised by punishment also generalize, poisoning the child's feelings about the sport itself as well as his or her liking of the coach. Eventually, both the coach and the sport itself generate such strong bad feelings that the child no longer wishes to participate and drops out of the sport. Many people never find other physical activities to replace the abandoned sport, contributing to the lack of exercise of Americans.

Some years ago I was at a Pony League Baseball game in a meaningless tournament, watching my then 8-year-old son's team play. The coach's son was on third base, my son was batting, it was the bottom of the last inning, and the score was tied with only one out. My son hit a rather weak grounder toward first, which managed to hit a lump of dirt on the base path and bounce sideways, slipping just past the first baseman's glove and stopping just behind him in the outfield. The first baseman recovered it quickly, but too late to step on the base. The coach's son immediately took off for home, the first baseman threw the ball, and the coach's son slid just under the tag, winning the game. The kids poured off the bench, pounding the coach's kid on the back and cheering, the kids lined up and slapped hands, and both teams returned to the dugout, our kids all smiles. The coach sat them all down, then turned to his son, glaring. "Did I tell you to run?" he said. "Did I give the run sign?" The kid looked at him blankly.

"I don't know," he finally mumbled.

"That's 'cause I didn't! You almost got tagged out! You should have gotten tagged out!" he growled. He poked a finger in his son's chest. "Next time I tell you to hold, you hold! Or you'll be riding the bench." He then turned and stalked out, leaving a silent bunch of 8-year-olds to clean up the equipment, none of them looking at the coach's son, who in turn was looking down with silent tears sliding down his face. He left the dugout eventually, shoulders slumped, his moment of triumph turned into something else. I wondered, then, how much longer he'd play baseball. I don't actually know, because we changed leagues after that, and I lost track of the family. But it doesn't take many negative experiences associated with an activity before one starts dreading it.

What could the coach have done instead? He could have let that moment go, not commented on it at all, let his son enjoy his triumph, and then watched for a chance in subsequent practices or games to point out when his son or a fellow teammate followed the signs and strongly praise that action. Both the child being praised for following the run and hold signs and the children who saw that child being praised would be more likely to follow the signs in the future, and as the kids increased the behavior of following the signs, the behavior of ignoring them would have declined. Even more important, the praise would have increased the children's liking of the game and their desire to do well, and would have increased their liking of the coach as well.

Most of the best professional sports managers and coaches have the lightest hands, quietly encouraging extra effort, ignoring mistakes and blunders or treating them as evidence that more opportunities are needed to build that skill (i.e., more practice). A good coach, a good mentor, and a good parent all lean most heavily on reinforcement and use punishments as sparingly as possible. In addition, a good coach, mentor, or parent also will focus on effort, not outcomes. Outcomes don't actually need our assistance to affect children's behaviors—they're naturally reinforced and punished. The kid who swings hard and hits the home run is reinforced by the home run itself and by teammate and crowd reactions—he or she doesn't need coaches or parents to point out the behavior was a good one. And the kid who watches a called third strike for the final out of the game is punished by the outcome itself and by the teammate and crowd reaction—he or she doesn't need coaches or parents to point out that waiting to walk wasn't a wise behavior in that situation. When children need us is when they try hard and the outcome still isn't favorable. That's when our reinforcement is most essential—when they swing their hardest and miss, when that pass slips through their outstretched fingers, or when they give it their all and still end up in the list of "also in the 100 yard dash were..." category. That's when they need to hear us say, "good try—I could see you did your best," or "good swing—next time you'll connect."

Can you teach an old dog new tricks either literally or metaphorically? Absolutely. But you have to focus your teaching efforts primarily on reinforcements or reinforcements, and use punishments as sparingly as possible (your ultimate goal should be to use no punishments at all). You also have to recognize that reciprocal control is the rule in human interactions—other people manipulate you as much as you manipulate them, even when we're talking about very, very young people. Everyone serves as both the puppet master and the puppet (none of us are Pinocchio, who had no strings). Most importantly, remember that you can catch more flies with honey than with vinegar.

References:

Bandura, A. (1973). *Aggresssion: A social learning analysis.* Englewood Cliffs, NJ: Prentice-Hall.

Bandura, A. (1997). *Self-efficacy: the exercise of control.* New York: Freeman.

Bjork, D. W. (1997) *B. F. Skinner: A life.* Washington, D. C.: American Psychological Association.

Skinner, B. F. (1971). *Beyond Freedom and Dignity.* Indianapolis: Hackett Publishing.

Skinner, B. F. (1948). *Walden Two.* Indianapolis: Hackett Publishing.

Thoreau, H. D. (1854). *Walden, or, Life in the Woods.* Boston: Ticknor and Fields.

Thorndike, E. L. (1911/1970). *Animal intelligence: Experimental studies.* New York: Macmillan.

Watson, John B. (1930). *Behaviorism*. Chicago: University of Chicago Press.

Chapter 5: Male and Female: Vive la Difference!

"I was asked if I feel like a woman now - but the truth is I have always felt like a woman - I just ended up in the wrong body." Kim Petras, one of the first people to delay puberty in order to perform sex reassignment surgery.

"I knew a transsexual guy whose only ambition is to eat, drink, and be Mary." Comedian George Carlin

The Origins of Sex

Let's say you decide to do your bit for the expansion of the human race and the perpetuation of your genes. After a roughly nine month gestational period, the magic day arrives and a new baby along with it. You'll forgive me, I hope, if I gloss over the details of the herculean efforts that are necessary on the part of the females of our species for making this miraculous thing happen. Believe me, you folks' contributions to this process are deeply appreciated by those of us who get to stand idly by and say things like, "You go, girl!" but that particular wondrous process isn't the focus of this narrative. And it's not because the male contribution to this whole enterprise, however necessary and pleasurable, is minimal and fleeting, let alone because we suffer from "womb envy." It's just that it's the product of this whole operation we're concerned with in this chapter, not the process by which that product came into being. (Besides, let's face it – the idea that males suffer from womb envy is as ludicrous as Freud's insistence that females have "penis envy." The short answers to both these claims are that we don't and you don't, either. But unless you're reading this the chapters of this book in a random or capricious order, you've probably already read about this issue in Chapter 1: *Freudian Hangovers*.)

So you and your partner become fruitful and multiply. You have the baby (You go girl!) or assist someone else in having the baby (primarily by looking sympathetic), and you spend some quiet minutes with this tiny new miracle. But then, traditionally, it's time for the person who didn't actually have to do any panting and pushing to begin calling friends and relatives in order to give them the good news. What's the first thing that the person on the other end of the line is going to want to know?

That's an easy one. "Is it a boy or a girl?" will probably be the very first question that you're asked, that is, unless you open the conversation by proclaiming, "it's a boy!" or "it's a girl!" yourself. This particular information will probably be passed on before vital statistics like weight and height, or even reassurances that proud, exhausted Mom is doing fine. Yet, if you think about it, at this particular moment, just after birth, the sex of the new person isn't an immediately important or terribly relevant thing for all our friends and relatives to know. By and large, the new baby is not going to be cared for any differently by others or behave any differently or have any different needs no matter what sex he or she is, at least not any time soon. Your new baby is going to be fed and changed and talked to, and will sleep 18 hours a day, and will scream in the middle of the night, and will need to be bathed and lotioned and held and cuddled, and none of these things are going to be materially different whether he is a he or she is a she.

But that simple fact doesn't matter to the any of us. The people around your new baby, including you, will treat him or her differently right from the outset of life based on the answer to that fundamental first question. They'll bring clothing with primary colors for your son, pastels for your daughter. They'll bring footballs he won't be able to grasp for months for your son, and pretty little bows for your daughter's virtually nonexistent hair. They'll tell you that your son looks strong and active and that your daughter is beautiful and sweet, and they'll believe it, and so will you, because they know boys are supposed to be strong and active and girls are supposed to be beautiful and sweet. And that's just the beginning. The older your child gets, the more differently we treat the boys and the girls.

The sense of being a male or a female, a boy or a girl, a man or a woman, is called one's sexual identity by some people, and one's gender identity by others. There is something of a war going on between groups of people concerning which term to use. The people favoring the term "gender identity" argue that we're talking about fundamental aspects of the person, not just sexual things, and that to call it "sexual identity" would be to focus too much on that narrow aspect of the concept. The people favoring the term "sexual identity" argue just as fervently that it is the sex of the person we're talking about here, not some esoteric label that was originally used to refer to categories in linguistics. In keeping with the argument I suggested in Chapter 2 of the first volume of this series, *Psychology in Plain English*, when I talked about linguistic superstition, I honestly don't believe that the exact term that one uses really matters. What really matters is that you understand what I mean by the term I use when I use it. So I'm going to use the term I prefer, "sexual identity," throughout this narrative. And to make sure there are no misunderstandings, I'm going to spend half of this chapter explaining what I mean by that term when I use it to refer to this vital aspect of our personalities.

So what's the basis of sexual identity? Most people will say that's easy—boys have male genitals, and girls have female genitals. That's a simple criterion, it's the criterion both you and your doctor used upon the birth of your child, and in most cases it leads us to a safe and reliable conclusion. But, depending upon various complicated circumstances, it's not always the right basis for conclusion, and to explain why it's not always the basis for conclusion we have to go right to the roots of sexual identity. How do we end up with male or female genitals to start with, and thus male or female bodies? Most people who have taken high school biology will probably say that all parts of our bodies, including our genitals, are a product of our chromosomes. Humans have 23 pairs of chromosomes, one set of 23 from each parent. The first 22 pairs are called autosomes and determine the characteristics of a wide variety of body parts and processes. The 23rd pair are called sex chromosomes because they tend to differ in males and females. Most femalcs have two large chromosomes for this pair that are the same size, but males have one large and one small chromosome. The large chromosomes are called X chromosomes, whereas the small chromosome normally found only in males is called a Y chromosome.

It's not the entire Y chromosome that determines the whether the person will have male or female genitals, though. It's merely a single gene on that chromosome that's responsible, a gene known as SRY-1. This gene tells your body how to make a protein known as the testis-differentiating factor (TDF), and production of TDF usually makes the developing embryo follow the male pattern of development.

Let's take a look more specifically at how this happens, because knowledge of the process is going to be important for us to fully understand the basis of sexual identity. SRY-1 has its effect during the early stages of embryonic development in the uterus. Around 6 weeks or so into gestation, if SRY-1 is present, it turns on and begins making TDF. TDF, in turn, alters the structure of the tiny, primitive gonads in the abdomen of the developing embryo, changing them into proto-testes. Those proto-testes, once they have developed to a certain point, begin secreting two hormones in quantities sufficient to affect the tiny embryonic body, Mullerian inhibiting hormome, and testosterone. Mullerian inhibiting hormone blocks growth of tissue that would become internal female genitals, and testosterone masculinizes the rest of the genitals as well as portions of the brain. By the time the process is done, you've got yourself a baby boy (nothing wrong with that).

You probably remember, from high school biology, that before sperm and egg cells are produced in the process of meiosis, the corresponding chromosomes from each parent get together and exchange parts with each other, scrambling our genes so that the sperm and egg cells we produce are all different, genetically, from each other. This is a process called "crossing over." But if you're a male person, the X and Y chromosome are different enough that they don't participate in crossing over (whereas the two X chromosomes in females do). So SRY-1 tends to stay on the Y chromosome, and thus if the embryo has a Y chromosome, it's almost always present and triggers the transformation of that embryo into a male. If the new embryo has two X chromosomes, though, SRY-1 is almost always absent, and thus the testis differentiating factor isn't produced and the gonads of the embryo continue down the female route, becoming ovaries. As ovaries rather than testes, they produce no Mullerian inhibiting hormone, so the internal female genitals aren't blocked from developing, and thus the fallopian tubes, uterus, and vagina form. The ovaries produce no testosterone either, so the external genitals aren't masculinized and neither is the brain, and we end up with a baby girl (nothing wrong with that, either).

So a male is someone with an X and a Y chromosome, and a female has two X chromosomes, right? That's certainly what international sports organizations maintained for a number of years. To make sure that the boys didn't try to compete with the girls, they would take cheek scrapings from competitors and subject them to chromosomal analysis, labeling the XY people males and the XX people females. This is a bit more complicated than the obstetrician's method of just visually inspecting the plumbing, but it's also a whole lot less embarrassing and intrusive for adult athletes. And in most cases, it comes out with the same results as visual inspection, plus it can unearth those who might be trying to slip by through the creative use of surgery. But chromosomal analysis causes a whole new set of problems. Because there are people whose chromosomes don't agree with their bodily appearances, even when no surgery is involved. In such cases, which indicator should we go by?

Let's take a look at some of the situations where a person's possession of two X chromosomes or and X and a Y chromosome may not match the person's resulting body. We'll start with the people who have genetic mutations of SRY-1, such that the gene itself is defective and doesn't make functional versions of the testis differentiating factor, as well as the people whose Y chromosome lacks SRY-1 entirely. In both these cases, these people will not make TDF to alter their developing gonads to follow the testicular route, so they won't make Mullerian inhibiting hormone or testosterone while developing in the uterus, and thus they'll end up with bodies that at birth appear female even though they have an X and a Y chromosome, even down to possessing a vagina and uterus. But because normal ovarian development requires a synergy between two functional X chromosomes, such females tend to have non-functional ovaries and generally do not undergo puberty without supplemental hormone therapy, and they'll be sterile. Bodily, they look like other females at birth. More relevant to sports competition, they would have no particular edge in strength or size or endurance over other women, either. But world sports organizations using chromosomal analysis would classify these people as males.

Then we have the inverse of the situation described above, people who have two X chromosomes, one of which has quite accidentally picked up SRY-1 from a Y chromosome. These people do produce the testis differentiating factor even though they have two X chromosomes, and in turn they masculinize their bodies like other boys and appear no different from other boys at birth. But because other genes normally found on the Y chromosome and not the X play roles in fertility and pubertal development, XX males generally have small genitals and tend to be sterile (not the sort of thing one usually notices until adulthood). By world sports standards based on chromosomes, they would have been classified as women despite their bodily appearances.

So far, we've seen that we can't necessarily judge sexual identity by people's genitals, and we can't necessarily judge it by people's gross chromosome complement, either. It's the presence or absence of a single gene, SRY-1, that usually determines if people have male or female bodies, not the entire Y chromosome. And that's just the beginning of the complications of this issue. Because it's also possible that SRY-1 might be present but not masculinize the body, or that SRY-1 will be absent but the body will be masculinized anyway, creating people whose genitals tend to appear contradictory not just with their chromosomes, but with that important gene. The most common of these situations involves people with *androgen insensitivity syndrome*. These are XY individuals with defects in the gene that makes cells recognize the hormone testosterone. Because the cells of these individuals don't recognize testosterone, they don't masculinize their bodies during the embryonic period, and they're born with external genitals that appear female, at least at first glance. But because they made Mullerian inhibiting hormone just like other males, they have no internal female genitals – no internal vagina, no uterus, and no fallopian tubes. They have immature, undescended internal testes, but the Wolffian bodies that form the other connective male structures such as the vas deferens remain vestigial. In addition, the brain structures that control sexual orientation and sex drive remain unmasculinized, because they're insensitive to testosterone as well, so these folks are usually attracted to males, generally feel like female people, and settle fairly easily into the female role. Lacking a uterus, they can't have babies, of course, and they'll need estrogen supplements at puberty. They'll also need surgery to create the missing internal vagina, and they'll never have menstrual periods. But otherwise they're normal appearing females despite the fact they have Y chromosomes.

There's a female counterpart to this situation as well. A number of normal XX female embryos are accidentally masculinized in the uterus. This may happen because the mother was exposed to high levels of testosterone through some bizarre environmental accident. It may also happen if the mother is given drugs that make her increase her own testosterone output. Alternatively, exposure to excess testosterone can also happen if the mother develops an adrenal gland tumor. Although often called a "male" hormone, testosterone is a vital hormone for both sexes. It's responsible for body hair and for sex drive, among other things. So both sexes make testosterone. In males, it is the testes that perform this task, but in females testosterone is made by the adrenal glands, a pair of endocrine glands that perch above the kidneys (hence the name "adrenal," as in "ad-renal" or, literally, "by the kidney" in Latin). Adrenal tumors often result in a vast increase in testosterone production, to a level that normally would not be seen in a female. If Mom just happens to be pregnant at that time, the embryo could be exposed to enough testosterone to alter its developmental course.

Whichever one of the three things listed above happens, if the embryo is exposed to sufficient testosterone, it can be masculinized even though the individual has two normal X chromosomes. In this case, though, only the external genitals and brain masculinize. Because the fetus does not have SRY-1 and thus does not produce the testis differentiating factor, it has internal ovaries. Those ovaries, in turn, do not produce Mullerian inhibiting hormone the way fetal testes would, so the fetus grows a normal uterus, fallopian tubes, and internal vagina that dead ends against the abdominal wall just behind the scrotum. Externally, the fetus looks like a boy with undescended testes. Internally, it's completely female. Often, though, people who receive enough testosterone to masculinize the fetus also have masculinized the brain, and they feel like normal boys as they go through childhood. Many don't even know of their intersex condition until they reach puberty and their ovaries start secreting estrogen, causing them to start growing breasts and sometimes triggering menstrual bleeding. With a little surgery to remove the unwanted female internal organs, and some prosthetic testicular implants, they often settle very nicely into male roles (although of course they're sterile, and they have to take supplemental testosterone to trigger genital growth, to grow and maintain body hair, and masculinize the larynx and other sexually dimorphic body parts).

Then there's another group. Any of the people described above might get caught in between, becoming boys or girls who are partially masculinized. Depending on how you look at it, they have partially closed labia or an incompletely closed scrotum, and they have an enlarged clitoris or a micropenis with an incompletely closed urethra. At birth the answer to the question of whether they are boys or girls isn't immediately clear by observation alone, and

it may not be clear even after they've been taken away and examined in detail by experts. Such children are often called "intersex" children. With them, the question becomes whether or not the brain was masculinized enough that they'll feel more like boys or more like girls. This is not something that can be resolved any time soon after birth. Children usually have to get to early childhood before they'll start showing a preference for playing with one sex rather than the other, for labeling themselves consistently as one sex and not the other, and, in the case of boys, desiring to urinate standing up. In the past, physicians would routinely assign the child to whatever sex it was easiest to surgically alter the child to resemble. This often worked well enough, because people whose bodies were masculinized enough to easily convert into boys usually had brains that were masculinized as well. And those whose bodies weren't masculinized very much also usually had brains that weren't masculinized, either, and thus they felt like girls as well.
Still, there were exceptions -- the rush to assign the child to a sex had its casualties. Sometimes the children who had been surgically feminized, once they reached childhood, felt distinctly like males despite their bodily indications, and those who had been assigned as males felt quite clearly like females once they got well into childhood. For these people, the expedient gender assignment at birth had clearly been the wrong choice, and now there was the problem of undoing previous surgery and changing a lifetime of labels.

In reaction to these significant failures to assign gender correctly and the consequences that ensued, these days physicians often aren't so quick to make arbitrary sex assignments and do surgery on these intersex children. Instead, they advise parents to give the child a preliminary label of sex assignment, but to avoid any surgery or other drastic actions until the child develops a strong sense of being male or female for long enough we're sure we've made the right choice. As most hormonal intervention and surgery can be put off until the date of normal puberty, the only complication this course of action creates is a need to backtrack to relatives and friends if the initial assignment of sex was wrong, but that's far less problematic than a rush to surgery would have been.

Now we'll move on to the most interesting group of all in this whole discussion of male and female. Unlike the people we've been talking about up to this point, people whose chromosomes don't agree with their bodies, this group of people have bodies that match their chromosomes. They're normal appearing XX females and normal appearing XY males. At birth, there's no question which sex they are. Their problem comes in when they get into the childhood years. That's when this group of people come to realize that they don't feel like the sex that their chromosomes and their bodies suggest that they are, but instead firmly feel that they are the opposite sex. Psychologists call these people transsexuals.

Transsexuals

Most people assume that transsexuals, people who feel like a male trapped in a female body or a female trapped in a male body, have some sort of mental illness. If your mind doesn't match your chromosomes or your body, there's got to be something wrong with your mind, they reason. Obligingly, the Diagnostic and Statistical Manual, Version IV, Text Revision (otherwise known as the DSM-IV-TR, or the Bible of mental illness), has a category relevant to transsexuals. It's labeled Gender Identity Disorder.

Now let me state at the outset that not all transsexuals have Gender Identity Disorder. There are two criteria for the diagnosis of Gender Identity Disorder on the DSM-IV-TR, both of which have to be present for the person to be so classified. The first criterion is the presence of transsexuality. But to have Gender Identity Disorder a person must also show the second criterion, and it's the one that's trickier. To be said to have gender identity disorder, the individual must also show great and persistent discomfort or distress with their transsexuality.

The first criterion isn't particularly hard to diagnose nor particularly controversial. You don't have to be a diagnostician on the level of the fictional Dr. Gregory House to identify the situation where, anatomically, a person's body is clearly and unequivocally one sex, yet the person also doesn't feel like that sex at all and never has. It's the second criterion that's complicated. One has to consider how one determines if a person has a persistent discomfort with his or her physical sexuality, and whether that discomfort is significant. Then, just to add another complication to the issue, we have to ask ourselves, just what is the source of this discomfort? Does the person have a disorder, or does their discomfort have some other source? Or is their problem a mismatch between their own natural characteristics and the demands of society, what Thomas Szasz called, in his seminal paper *The Myth of Mental Illness*, "problems in living?" (Szasz, 1960).

Our usual reaction to people whose sexual identity doesn't match their bodies is inherent in our ways of thinking about the world. As human beings, we don't like things that are inconsistent, and things that are indeterminate. Human beings like to put things into nice, neat categories. Once we do, we believe we know how to deal with those things, we think we know what to expect of them, and we delude ourselves into thinking we understand them. If we've decided that the creature that Lutwidge is leading toward us on a leash is a dog, we think we know where we stand. We feel we know what to expect of the creature, we assume we know how to interact with it, and we think we understand it. But if we weren't able to categorize the creature, we'd probably be puzzled, uncomfortable, or even fearful. Heck, it's possible that the creature approaching us is dangerous in some unanticipated way. As a consequence, we are highly eager to make new things fit our categories, if for no other reason than reassurance. Yet in simplifying the world, we also may be forcing some things into categories where they don't fit all that well, and we may end up insisting two things be the same even when they clearly not the same at all.

Consider what happens when it's clear that a thing doesn't fit into our categories at all. We are left with two possibilities both disturbing – that there's something wrong with our categories, or that there's something wrong with the thing that doesn't fit our categories. Challenges to our categories are challenges to our world views, and require us to do some serious rethinking. We hate challenges to our world views, and we hate rethinking. What we generally do rather than these two effortful, hated activities is to blame the thing that doesn't fit rather than our erroneous categories. "That thing is different!" we say in wounded outrage. "It's wrong! It doesn't fit our view of the world! It must be changed!"

This is very much the case when we talk about sexual identities of people. We classify the people of the world into boys and girls, men and women, generally based on bodily appearance, and then we relax, comfortable that we know what sort of person we're dealing with and what to expect of them. We then expect all the aspects of the person's sex to match those of one of our neat little pair of sexual categories.

But although sexuality begins in sexual identity, it doesn't end there, and many other things depend on that sexual identity. There are four other aspects to people's sexuality besides sexual identity, and, while the five of them may more or less match in most people, they don't necessarily totally match in everyone. (Seligman, et al., 2001). Some of these are deep and unchangeable, some of more flexible. These consist, in order from deepest to shallowest, of sexual identity, sexual orientation, sexual interests or preferences, sex roles, and sexual performance. To more fully understand upcoming portions of our discussion, we'll have to do a quick detour to look at each of these aspects, then we'll be able to return to our discussion of transsexuality.

The deepest level of sexuality is sexual identity, the very issue we've been discussing up to this point. Sexual identity involves whether you feel like a male or female person. From the point of view of psychologists, whichever sex you feel like is your sexual identity, whether or not that feeling matches the appearance of your body or your chromosomes. Thus, in each of the complicated conditions we discussed at the beginning of the chapter, the persons' sexual identities were always which sex they felt like once they got to an age when they were aware of such feelings, regardless of what their bodies or their chromosomes suggested.

Sexual orientation, the next level up, involves which sex you're most closely attracted to. Although most people view sexual orientation as a dichotomy, suggesting you're either attracted to the opposite sex or your own sex, or a trichotomy, where you're attracted to your own sex, the opposite sex, or equally to both sexes, it's probably more accurate to see sexual orientation as a continuum. The continuum of sexual orientation ranges from exclusive heterosexuality at one end to exclusive homosexuality at the other, with varying degrees of each as we move across the continuum. So to classify one's sexual orientation would involve determining which sex is your favorite, even if it's just by a little bit. The only way to know someone's sexual orientation would be to have access to their fantasies. Suppose you were to fantasize the most erotic, wonderful, perfect sexual encounter that you could imagine—sex that would be just perfect for you if you could just make that happen. Your sexual orientation is revealed by the sex of your partner in that fantasy scenario. If it's the opposite sex from your gender identity, then you're a heterosexual. If it's the same sex as your own identity, then you're a homosexual. And if you could literally flip a coin and the other person's sex didn't matter, you'd be bisexual. Bear in mind that the odds of the latter are almost nil. There would be very few situations where we could legitimately say that a person was bisexual —almost everyone has some preference for one sex or the other, even if it's very slight.

Lay people often use the term "bisexual" to refer to people who've had sexual experience with both sexes. Who you're actually having sex with is a sexual performance issue, not an issue of sexual orientation. People can often engage in sex of a type that isn't their preferred thing, and thus might have experience with both sexes. But they are probably still attracted more to one sex than the other, and thus they remain heterosexual or homosexual despite who they're having sex with at a given time. Thus, we should probably talk about "bisexual behavior," in such a situation, not "bisexual people."

Sexual interests are the particular situations, types of people and scenarios you find most sexually exciting. Sexual interests are often mundane – most people are attracted to similar types of things. Females tend to be attracted to strong chins and broad shoulders, and males tend to be attracted to shapely hips, prominent breasts, and softer facial features. But beyond that there is tremendous variation. Some people like mustaches and some don't, and some like larger or smaller breasts, particular hair colors, or particular situations. Some people are into rarer things like pirate scenarios, or playing the naughty schoolboy and the strict school marm, or peeping into other people's windows. The range of sexual interests is quite frankly mind-boggling, and you'd probably be astounded were you to find out the sexual interests of your friends, neighbors, coworkers, and relatives (and possibly baffled or even horrified as well, depending on how different they are from your own sexual interests).

Where do these sexual interests come from? Sexual interests have some biological basis in that we're inclined somewhat toward the attributes of the sex that is the target of our particular sexual orientations, but they also have a large learned component. It appears that when we first start feeling powerful sexual drives, early on in adolescence, we tend to associate attributes of our first sexual experiences with that powerful sexual arousal, making those things strongly sexual in nature. If we then repeat the pairing of those characteristics of the person or situation with arousal in subsequent fantasies, those attributes become sexual interests. So we might go through life lusting after guys with glasses like that boy you first fumbled around with, or girls wearing high heels like the one at the junior high dance who brushed against you in such a provocative fashion.

Sex roles are your public expression of being a male or female person, including things like dress, hair styles, and professional and leisure time activities. To some degree sex roles have a biological basis. Boys tend to adopt more aggressive sex roles than girls because of the effects of testosterone, for example, and because of that same hormone boys tend to wander more and twitch around more than girls even when they're sitting still. Girls tend to focus more on seeking consensus in the group rather than competing with others, and can sit still for hours if they're engrossed in something (Money, 1986). Other evidence that some sex roles are influenced by biology can be found in studies where testosterone-reducing hormones were given to pregnant women. The boys born of those women played less stereotypic masculine games than other boys, and the girls born of them played more feminine games than other girls (Meyer-Bahlburg, et al., 1988). Beyond such biological inclinations, though, most sex roles are arbitrary and culturally-based. Hair length, type and style of jewelry, clothing styles, and many of the other superficial aspects of sex roles vary widely from culture to culture and are learned from the other males and females around us.

Many people confuse sex roles with sexual orientation, assuming that homosexual males adopt more feminine sex roles and homosexual females adopt more masculine ones, so they expect male homosexuals to be “swishy” and female homosexuals to be “butch.” These affectations, though, are sex roles, and thus like the sex roles of heterosexual males and females, are a combination of biology and experience. Some homosexual males may avoid more violent games and roam less, for example, because of different hormonal effects on the brain in utero, but others may simply model their sex roles after other homosexual males who follow this pattern. Some homosexual females may adopt a more masculine sex role because of hormonal effects in utero, but others may simply be imitating adult role models for homosexual females. The majority of homosexuals, both male and female, maintain the sex roles of their heterosexual peers, and thus behave no differently in following their sex roles than any other males or females. There are some subcultures, in fact, where homosexuals deliberately take an opposing tack in their sex roles, with homosexual males acting even more macho than the average heterosexual man, and female homosexuals behaving even more femininely than the average heterosexual woman (Connell, 2005).

Sexual performance is actual ability to function sexually in situations that call for sexual functioning. One of the things people often don't realize is that sexual performance is quite separable from the other aspects of people's sexuality. You may be attracted to a particular sex and have interests in that particular person and still be unable or unwilling to perform sexually. Likewise, most people are flexible enough to perform sexually even if the partner doesn't match their particular sexual interests, and some can perform even if the partner doesn't match their sexual orientation! Many homosexuals can perform sexually with opposite sex partners. It's just not their favorite thing. And many heterosexuals can, in a pinch, perform with same sex partners, especially on long sea voyages, when no other more suitable partner is available, or simply when desire becomes strong enough that it trumps preferences (the phrase "horny teen-ager" comes to mind, because many people experiment with types of sex that aren't their favorite thing in adolescence and early adulthood before settling down into a steady pattern of sexual behavior of a particular type once sex of that type is possible and readily available).

That's the short story on the five layers of sexuality. You can see, with five layers of sexuality, that there are actually quite a few ways for the person's body to fail to match some aspect of their sexuality. They aren't all equally troubling to others, though. The shallower aspects of sexuality vary quite extensively from one male or female to another, so when people don't match our gender expectations on them, it doesn't bother us as much. A man or woman might not be all that interested in sex with a particular person at the moment, but we still don't consider this variation to indicate that they aren't men or women. People may dress androgynously or act outside their sex roles, and we still see them as men and women (although if their actions or dress get very far outside the norm for their sex, it starts bothering people). Sexual interests can cause troubles when they are acted upon if they are very different from your sexual identity or very different from the mundane interests of most other people, but if they remain in your head as fantasies, they generally cause no problems at all no matter how odd they are.

Moving deeper into your sexuality, when your sexual orientation doesn't match your bodily appearance, as is the case for homosexuals, some people are bothered quite a bit, whereas others don't really care. Those who care appear to care a great deal and are very vocal about it, sometimes to homicidal levels. Those who don't really care about other people's sexual orientations generally argue that we're talking about behavior that generally takes place in private and involves only consenting partners, and thus really doesn't affect anyone else.

That leaves us with gender identity. We expect that people with male genitals will feel like males, will be attracted to female people, will have male sexual interests, and will adopt male sex roles and do what we consider are male things. We expect people with female genitals will feel like females, will be attracted to male people, will have female sexual interests, and will adopt female sex roles and will do what we consider female things. We can ignore the other four aspects of sexuality when they don't fit a person's body, because they're either qualities that often vary between males and between females anyway, or they're private activities, not right there in front of us, mocking our classification system. But people who have male bodies but feel like female people, or people who have female bodies but feel like male people are a fundamental challenge to our classification system. No part of their sexuality fits our neat little categories. Yet the bodies that they're in aren't something we can ignore—they're right out there in the open, continuously reminding us that the person's identity doesn't match that body. The net result is that our inability to classify these folks really, really bugs some people.

But if you're the one who doesn't fit the categories, does that make you the problem? To go further, does that make you mentally ill? Let's go back to the DSM-IV-TR. Remember that there are two criteria that must be met in the diagnosis of gender identity disorder. Being a transsexual (having a body that doesn't match your sexual identity) is half of the diagnosis, but a DSM-IV-TR diagnosis of Gender Identity Disorder requires that the person also have persistent discomfort with that transsexual bodily identity. That's where the diagnostic problems begin, problems similar to those we discussed in Chapter 4 of the previous volume of this series, *Psychology in Plain English*, for ADHD and for reading disorder. Just how much discomfort must one experience before it's persistent discomfort? Casually wishing one's body was different is a very different thing from hating one's body with a passion. Heck, I casually wish my body was different (as in less prone to accumulating body fat and not quite so old-, wrinkled-, and bald-looking) now and then. How intense does this wishing have to be before it becomes persistent discomfort? And how much of the discomfort of the transsexual person is due to the fact that we're trying to classify the person into a category and insisting that he or she behave certain ways that fit that classification? How many of their problems, how much of their distress, and how much of their discomfort is due to the fear of being found out, being rejected, being fired, being discriminated against, or even being bodily assaulted, or simply being viewed as a freak rather than with the fact of transsexuality itself?

One of the difficulties with all of this is our general attitude that, when things don't fit our categories, it's the things that are at fault, not the categorization system. Some people even view all transsexuals as being deliberately difficult, insisting on a contrary gender identity just to get attention or irritate other people. Fundamentally, they're blaming the victims. Such people don't care that years of research has demonstrated about as thoroughly as one can expect science to demonstrate such things that people don't choose gender identity and it doesn't appear to be influenced by rearing, either (Zucker & Bradley, 1995).

Even psychologists aren't totally free of blame from such beliefs. It wasn't all that long ago that some were claiming quite adamantly that it was how children were treated in early childhood that determined gender identity, and those old beliefs are hard to shake. Sigmund Freud, for example, argued that the resolution of his fanciful Oedipal complex determined gender identity, and blamed gender identity problems in both sexes on children having a weak father and an overly strong mother. More recently, prominent sex researcher John Money was still insisting that early and consistent gender labeling when children were young was behind gender identity, and that gender identity disorder was merely a failure of this labeling. Call a child a boy or a girl consistently before the school years, Money believed, and that's who he or she would feel like for life (Money & Erhardt, 1972).

Freud did his work a long time ago, and thus isn't as influential today. But Money's body of work still influences many. In one of the more unusual ironies of the history of psychology, Money also provided one of the strongest collections of supporting evidence that his theory that early and consistent labeling of sex was responsible for sexual identity was dead wrong. Both the misconception and the more recent refutation of it is a result of the remarkable and extremely heartbreaking case of the opposite-sexed identical twins.

The Opposite-Sexed Identical Twins

Unless you're already familiar with this case, I bet that the last sentence of the previous section was a real attention-getter. How could people possibly be of opposite sexes and be identical twins? Here, we're using the common term "identical twins," to mean what are more specifically called "monozygotic twins," that is, twins who are the result of the splitting of a single zygote into two cells that grew into two separate individuals. Identical twins aren't, of course, completely identical, as anyone who's ever known such twins can testify. They often have subtle differences between them, the results of different experiences and mutations. But being of different sexes?

It happens. Rarely, but it happens. When it happens, it's generally because a single Y-chromosome-bearing zygote split right after conception, creating twin zygotes. But after the split, a mutation makes SRY-1 nonfunctional in one of the two zygotes that resulted from the twinning. The fetus with the mutated SRY-1 gene never undergoes fetal masculinization, resulting in twins who came from the same zygote and share almost all of the same genes but the critical one that would allow them to share the same genitals. You end up with opposite sexed "identical" twins. But these opposite sexed identical twins aren't the subject of our focus at the moment. When this happens, the twin with female appearing genitals invariably feels female, and the one with the male genitals feels male, so their brains and bodies match, even if the chromosomes of one twin don't match the body. And they're not really identical at birth – one clearly appears to be a boy, the other a girl. The case of opposite sexed identical twins that concerns us in this chapter is a more bizarre and tragic saga that was documented by Joseph

Colapinto in his book, *As Nature Made Him: The Boy who was Raised as a Girl* (2001) .

Back in 1965, Ron and Janet Reimer of Canada had a pair of normal identical twin boys, who they named Bruce and Brian. Because of repeated urinary tract infections that were difficult to treat, the hospital recommended the boys be circumcised some months after birth. (Whether treating constant urinary tract infections in boys is best handled by circumcision is beyond the scope of this discussion. In this particular case, though, the result was disastrous.) Through a series of improbable events that compounded one on top the other, Bruce's penis was completely burned to a crisp by an electric cauterizing device that shouldn't have been anywhere near such a simple operation to start with. Bruce was taken to one physician after another, all of whom reported there was nothing that could be done to restore the boy's penis and he would have to go through childhood without one (sexual reconstructive surgery was rudimentary at the time).

After despairing for some time, they heard Dr. John Money suggesting on a television program broadcast in Canada that gender identity was created by how children were raised and labeled during the first few years of life, and not by their biology. Money was contacted for help, and he agreed that poor, mutilated Bruce needn't be scarred for life. He informed the parents that, as a result of his research, he was pretty sure that if they were to surgically remove the boy's testes, do some surgery to create a semblance of a vulva, and raise this newly altered child as a girl, she would settle into that role easily and naturally. At puberty this now female person could receive hormone injections to cause breast growth and a feminine figure, vaginal construction could be accomplished to make sexual activity possible, and she would be just fine, or at least as fine as could be expected considering the circumstances.

So what could a parent do but agree? Money seemed competent and sure of himself, poor little Bruce was mutilated in what pretty much anyone would consider a most distressing and humiliating fashion, and there didn't seem to be any other alternative. Picturing all the heartache that being a boy with no penis would cause their son, the Reimers agreed, the surgery was done, and Bruce Reimer became Brenda Reimer.

Sadly, the results did not go as Money had predicted. Brenda Reimer did not settle easily into being a girl and wanting to do girl things. In fact, the result was quite the opposite – from the outset he didn't feel like a girl, he didn't want to play with girl things, he don't want to wear female clothing, and he didn't want to hang out with girls. He hated dressing up, and, to the consternation of both his mother and the other girls at school, he frequently urinated standing up, a position that he preferred despite the derision it brought down on him from all sides. He hung out with the boys, and he was quick with his fists if anyone took issue with his behavior or appearance. He constantly sat with his legs apart despite the negative reaction this caused from those around him, and he hated dresses with a passion.

Now you have to bear in mind that no one had told him he'd been born a boy, and as far as he knew he was a girl with a vague birth defect that made his genitals look a bit odd and that would require him to take hormones starting at puberty. Yet as he neared the age of puberty, and as his body was altered by hormone injections to appear more feminine, he become depressed to the point of being suicidal at the prospect of attaining a feminine figure. At the advice of his endocrinologist, it was finally disclosed to him by his father that he'd been born a boy and was, in fact, his brother's identical twin (by this point they didn't look all that identical due to Bruce/Brenda's lack of exposure to testosterone and due to the estrogen treatments). Upon hearing that he'd been born a boy, the sex he'd always felt he should be, Bruce/Brenda put his foot down, stopping his hormone treatments and saying that he did not, absolutely, positively did not want to be a girl any more. He started taking testosterone not long thereafter, had surgery to remove the breast tissue he'd hated from the moment it had started growing, received successful genital construction surgery, and began life thereafter as the male he'd always felt he was.

I wish I could say the story had a happy ending after all this suffering, but it doesn't. Bruce/Brenda changed his name to David and married a very understanding lady with some children of her own to whom he served as a stepfather. But the trauma of his childhood and being forced to try to fit a gender role that didn't match his brain left him bitter and extremely angry at Money, whose advice had subjected him to the problem to start with. He went public with his story, appearing on TV and in magazine articles, and had his story published by John Colapinto. He was bitter not only about his detested childhood, but about the fact that his testes had been removed and discarded back when he was a baby, so he couldn't even make his own testosterone naturally or father children, something he might have actually been able to do had Money's ill-advised course of action not been taken. This and many other factors in his life appear to have led him to depression and chronic unemployment. Adding to his troubles, his beloved twin brother developed schizophrenia and then apparently committed suicide by overdosing on his medications. He also apparently lost a large amount of money on an ill-fated investment. David became despondent, driving his wife to separate from him in what she saw as a temporary measure while he got his life back together again. He reacted by storming out of the house, but within days he returned, retrieved a shotgun, went to his workshop where he carefully and deliberately cut the barrel off the gun to shorten it, and drove to a local supermarket parking lot where he killed himself with the altered weapon.

David Reimer's story raised a necessary cautionary flag to all parents and physicians who feel compelled to do arbitrary gender assignment to children with ambiguous genitals at birth. But it also raised some interesting ethical problems concerning transsexual children and children with Gender Identity Disorder. Many psychologists argue that the biggest problems of transsexual children is not the mismatch between their sexual identities and their physical bodies. Instead, they argue, the biggest problems of transsexual children arise from the reactions of the people around them, the people who insist that their behaviors and identity match their bodies. Yet this is not a state of affairs that is going to be settled quickly—when transsexuals do have gender reassignment surgery, that surgery is not done until they are adults. This creates another problem many transsexuals find quite distressing—the prospect of going through puberty and developing an increasingly sexually dimorphic body—a body that gradually becomes more and more like the body of the sex they already do not identify with.

Bear in mind that all the evidence suggests that most transsexual children know, from the early school years, that they're not the boys or girls they bodily appear to be. They want to be like the other boys or girls that their brains insist they are, but their bodies make other people of that sex reject them, treat them differently and deny that they are kindred spirits. They may dislike their bodies to varying degrees to start with, but the reactions of others undoubtedly intensify these negative feelings. They'd like to live the lives of the sex that their brains say they are, but with their opposite sexed bodies other people won't let them. There's no possibility of them changing the way their brains make them feel—as near as we can tell, that's established by hormones in utero and never changes thereafter. Yet it will be many years before they can alter their bodies surgically to match the sex that they feel they are.

This is where the ethical complication came in. Sex change surgery cannot be done until the body fully matures. In addition, there are issues of whether younger people can be said to be competent enough to judge whether they really are trapped in the wrong body are not. And until recently, in the United States and in most other countries, physicians also would not hormonally delay puberty until children became old enough to voluntarily undergo sex change surgery. That meant that transsexuals, most of whom realize that they are transsexuals long before puberty, had to go through puberty and attain the differentiated adult physiques of the sex they don't want to be before we'd even discuss gender reassignment surgery with them.

Once those transsexuals reached adulthood, they were welcome to alter their own bodies, but most of the sexual dimorphism that comes with puberty was irreversible or at least not easily changed. People who feel like females but are in male bodies have to grow the large larynxes of males, huge man hands, broad shoulders, the rough skin of males along with males' copious and coarse body hair. People who feel like males in female bodies have to grow breasts, which they'd later have to have surgically removed, and the wider hips of females that will never look masculine when they finally do have the chance to have their bodies altered to embrace their mental pictures of themselves. They never had the chance to grow the strong jaw that most males have, or their large hands and feet, or their broad shoulders, because bone growth stopped long before they began taking the larger doses of testosterone that would make that happen. So once they finally did opt to alter their bodies to match their minds, transsexuals find the process has become much more complicated and the alterations much harder to satisfactorily complete.

Thus, not long ago in Germany, young Kim Petras, then 12 but already quite sure she was a transsexual with a male body but female identity, began testosterone blocking therapy to prevent the masculinizing effects of puberty, and began taking estrogen so that she could start the feminine contouring of her body and begin growing breasts on schedule. She then went public with her plea to obtain government permission for sex reassignment surgery to complete the process. She must have made a compelling case, because her request was granted, and at 16 she became the youngest person up to that point in Germany to receive gender reassignment surgery. The case created some controversy in Germany and a much bigger uproar in the U. S., with Internet sites calling her a "freak" and an "attention seeker." Most of these sites also condemned her parents and the health officials of Germany, and raged that children don't know what they want and shouldn't be allowed to make such critical decisions. Yet you can see Kim's reasoning quite clearly. She was proclaiming to her parents before preschool that she wasn't a boy and didn't want to be one, despite what her genitals suggested, and that feeling never changed in her throughout childhood. So why, she asked, should we insist that she go through the pubertal changes that will make her ability to live life as a female, the gender that her brain says she is, so much more difficult? Why couldn't she block male puberty before it altered her body to be even less like the body she feels she should have?

Yet you can see the other side to this argument. There are bound to be some people who simply are confused, and not at all sure whether they are really a person trapped in the body of the other sex or not. There are also bound to be people who are momentarily delusional, people who believe they are trapped in the wrong body due to high levels of suggestibility, people who simply desire attention, and people who are under great pressure from others to claim to be trapped in the wrong body. These people wouldn't make up even a substantial minority of those who claim to be transgendered people, but such people would pop up on occasion. It is not unreasonable to insist that individuals be mentally mature and very sure of their feelings about their bodily sex before embarking on sex reassignment surgery.

But delaying puberty for people like Kim Petras is a much less drastic step than full gender reassignment surgery, with little potential for long-lasting harm. That's one of the reason that Kim's pioneering treatment is quickly becoming more common in the United States as well as Europe. Juvenile transsexuals now face far fewer hurdles in obtaining hormone suppression therapy to hold off puberty until they are old enough to seek actual gender reassignment surgery, thus erasing one of the factors that increase dissatisfaction and distress among transsexuals.

For that matter, is it really necessary for transsexuals to get gender reassignment surgery in order to live fulfilling lives at all? Who would be harmed if transsexuals simply dressed and lived as the sex they feel they are, or got hormone therapy but stopped short of surgery, a surgery that carries with it the risk of damaging ability to orgasm? Would they be so upset about their cross-gendered bodies if we didn't react so negatively to them? Is gender identity disorder really a problem inherent in the person, or is it, as Thomas Szasz put it in our discussion in Chapter 4, of the previous volume of this series, *Psychology in Plain English*, a problem in living (Szasz, 1960)?

I don't really know the answer to that question, and neither does anyone else, because we don't live in a society where transsexuals are treated with such tolerance, and thus we can't know how much of their dissatisfaction is due to our reaction to their bodies rather than their bodies. I do know that sexuality isn't the "boy-girl" "man-woman" dichotomy that we insist upon imposing upon it. There are many aspects to our sexuality, and they don't necessarily coincide in any given person. Our sexual orientations may not match our sexual identities, our sexual interests may not correspond with either one, our sex roles are separate from all of them to a great degree, and sexual performance tells us little about the others. To try to encompass all of that in a term like "male" and "female" is as fruitless as trying to encompass the wonder of living things into the simple categories "plant" and "animal." There's a reason I entitled this chapter "Vive la Difference," a phrase whose origins are lost in the early part of the 20th century. Some report, though, that the phrase was the result of a discussion between an Englishman and a Frenchman over men and women and their places in life and society. "There is very little difference between men and women," the Englishman reportedly stated. "Vive la difference!" the Frenchman supposedly rejoined. I used the phrase to head this chapter, because I wanted to highlight the differences not between men and women or boys and girls, but between individuals within each of these supposedly different categories. I wanted to celebrate not just the wonderful dichotomy of male and female, but the incredible diversity of maleness and femaleness within each category. There are massive variations in how different men and different women experience sexuality, in their preferences, in their likes and dislikes, and in their secret fantasies. That variation means that, as my mom advised me years ago, there really is someone for everyone out there. Where would I be, after all, if my own dear and long suffering wife hadn't had a peculiar penchant for nerdy intellectual types who wear glasses?

References:

Colapinto, (2001). *As Nature Made Him: The Boy who was Raised as a Girl.* New York: Harper Perennial.

Connell, R.W. 2005. *Masculinities.* Sydney: Allen & Unwin.

Meyer-Bahlburg, H., Feldman, J., Cohen, P., & Ehrhardt, A. (1988). Perinatal factors in the development of gender-related play behavior: Sex hormones versus pregnancy complications. Psychiatry, *51*, 260-271.

Money, J. (1986). Venuses penuses: Sexology, sexosophy, & exingency theory. Buffalo, NY: Prometheus Books.
Money, J., & Ehrhardt, A. (1972). *Man and woman, boy and girl.* Baltimore: John Hopkins University Press.

Seligman, M. E. P., Walker, E. F., and Rosenhan, D. L. (2001). *Abnormal Psychology(4th Edition).* New York: Norton.

Szasz, Thomas. *(1960)* The myth of mental illness. *American Psychologist*, *15*, 113-118. Can also be retrieved from http://psychclassics.yorku.ca/Szasz/myth.htm

Teen sex swap girl talks. (2009). Article retrieved from: http://www.thesun.co.uk/sol/homepage/news/article2203926.ece?OTC-RSS&ATTR=News

Zucker, K. J., and Bradley, S. J. (1995) *Gender identity disorder and psychosexual problems in children and adolescents.* New York: Guilford Press.

Chapter 6: Accentuating the Positive

You've got to accentuate the positive, eliminate the negative, and latch on to the affirmative, don't mess with Mister In-Between. Popular Song of the 1940's

If you think you can do a thing or think you can't do a thing, you're right. Henry Ford

Death is easy. Comedy is hard. Quote of unknown origin attributed to many famous actors.

Controllability and Locus of Causality

Let's start out by imagining a scenario. You're at a big buffet, and you fill your tray with delicious food. Moving on to the drink counter, you grab the biggest glass they have available and fill it almost to the top with chocolate milk, the most delicious drink in the universe. Just as you're going to put it down, something hits both your elbows, driving your arms up and making you dump the entire glass of chocolate milk on yourself. Dripping and milk-besplotched, you turn around just in time to see a friend of yours directly behind you. "Gotcha," he says. (I made the evil friend male here because this sounds more like the sort of trick male friends would pull—females tend to be more indirect with their tricks. But feel free to substitute "she" in the story if your evil friends are female). So tell me. How do you feel as you're standing there, dripping?

My guess is that you're majorly ticked off. Quite stunningly angry. Ready to bite nails in half. Thoroughly and majorly peeved. Perhaps even bordering on homicidal. You went from happily anticipating a fine meal to sticky, cold, uncomfortable, and definitely not ready for prime time in seconds. I'm guessing the person who bumped your elbows had better be pretty fleet of foot, or able to take a punch.

Now let's change the scenario ever so slightly. We'll start the same way—you've just gotten your cacao-infused moo juice, you go to set it down, both your elbows are jolted, you dump it all over yourself, you turn—but this time, what you see isn't a friend saying, "Gotcha," but a fellow with leg braces trying to disentangle his crutches and get up again from where he fell, bumping you on the way down. You're still standing there, sticky, cold, uncomfortable, and definitely not ready for prime time. So tell me—how do you feel now?

You wouldn't think it would make any difference. You suffered the same consequences in both scenarios. You're just as harmed in both versions of the story, in both another person caused the harm, and in both you were an innocent victim. The milk is just as cold and wet, and you're just as much a spectacle in each story. Yet I bet your reaction to the second story was very different. Upon turning and seeing the cause of your discomfiture, what you'd probably feel in the second scenario isn't anger at the person who bumped you, but pity. You'd probably try to help him up, while muttering quick assurances such as, "No big deal—I'm washable," or "That's okay—it'll wipe off."

What this brief thought experiment demonstrates is that one of the biggest factors in our emotional reactions is our own thoughts about the experiences we have. We're especially swayed by three factors in determining what emotions we feel. The first is pretty straightforward—is the thing that happened a good or a bad thing?

Good things cause good emotions, and bad things cause bad. The second is what is known as "locus of causation," or, more simply, who caused the situation. The third is the degree of controllability itself—did the person have any other choice but to cause the situation? Was it on purpose, or was it an accident? Together, the answers to these three questions largely determine which emotions we're going to feel.

All of these are part of what scientists call "attribution theory." When events happen, we often make judgments about the causes or origins of those events, and the motivations of the people who engage in those events. Such judgments are called "attributions," because we're attributing behavior or motivation to a particular thing. The particular aspect of attribution theory we're examining here is the work of UCLA emeritus Dr. Bernard Weiner (Weiner, 1985). Let's take a look at Weiner's analysis of the particular emotions we are expected to feel when different combinations of these three factors occur.

Let's take a look, first, at situations like my first two examples, where a bad thing happens to you. The key considerations are who caused the bad thing to happen (locus of causality), and could they have avoided causing it to happen (controllability). In both of our examples, it was a person outside ourselves who caused the bad thing to happen, so the locus of causality was external to us. In the example when your friend was playing "Gotcha," the behavior was controllable on the part of that person—he didn't have to make us dump milk all over ourselves, but he chose to do so anyway. Weiner argued that when a bad thing is caused by someone else who could easily have avoided doing that bad thing, the emotion we feel is anger.

The second example, where the person with the leg braces fell off of his crutches also involves a bad thing being caused by someone else. But in this case, the event was uncontrollable. He or she could not help what happened and did not bump us deliberately, but did so accidentally. In such a situation where the bad thing is external to us and uncontrollable, Weiner argued that the emotion that is felt is pity, not anger. What's the difference between the two scenarios? Only our judgment of the controllability of the action. If we judge that the person harmed us and could have avoided it, we'll be angry, but if we think there was no way to avoid the harm, we feel pity. Note that we're not talking about the objective judgment of whether the action by the other person was controllable or not, we're talking about our own assessment of that action. Thus, if we incorrectly attribute lack of controllability to the person in the first example, or controllability to the second, we could very well feel emotions for the situation that others might deem inappropriate.

But how about the emotions of the person who caused you to dump milk all over yourself? What emotions should that person feel? Weiner's theory addresses that issue, too. In this case, though, the locus of control is internal, because we're looking at it from the perspective of the person who is causing the harmful event. Weiner argued that in our first scenario, the person who bumped your arms should feel guilty. The action was completely controllable—the person could opt to do it or not do it. He or she chose to do it, caused a bad outcome, and should feel guilt for having done so. Guilt, according to Weiner, has a reciprocal relationship with anger. In situations where one person is feeling anger because of the actions of another, we expect the person who was cause of the situation to feel guilt, and in situations where the cause of the situation feels guilt, he or she should expect the person who was harmed to feel anger. Indeed, the angry person is apt to feel more angry if the person who caused the situation doesn't feel guilt!

Now in our second scenario, Weiner argued that the person who caused the milk spill should feel shame, not guilt, because the action was uncontrollable. Our individual with the crutches and leg braces didn't mean to cause you to spill milk on yourself and didn't want it to happen. When the cause of a bad event is internal to you and uncontrollable, according to Weiner you should feel shame. The person who was the victim of the bad event, meanwhile, should feel pity in that same scenario. Overall, the outcomes look like this:

		Controllability	
		Uncontrollable	Controllable
Locus of Causation	External	Pity	Anger
	Internal	Shame	Guilt

When there is a lack of symmetry in the emotions of the victim and the person who caused the negative situation, it usually arises because there is a difference of opinion between the parties concerning just how controllable the situation was. This often takes the form of the person who caused the situation arguing that it wasn't controllable, and therefore the victim should not be angry but should feel pity instead, while at the same time the victim is arguing that the situation was controllable and that therefore the person who caused it should feel guilt.

What about situations where good things happen instead of bad things? Do locus of causation and controllability play roles there? Absolutely. Let's consider another scenario. You invite some people over for dinner at your house and decide to make your famous mock eggplant soup (now with more mock eggplant!).

You use your brilliant culinary expertise to pick the perfect ingredients, and chop them up using your knife that can cut through a tin can and still slice a tomato, the one that came with the Handy-Dandy Dust Bunny Fluffer you bought when you saw it advertised on late night TV. You then begin simmering and seasoning. You taste the soup again, decide it needs just a little bit of parsley, sage, rosemary, and thyme, and, voila! You've made the perfect soup. When you serve it to your guests, what emotion should you feel?

Pride, of course. You'll feel pride because, according to Weiner, that's the emotion one feels when a good thing happens that the person him or herself caused, and he or she had control over it, and thus had chosen what to put in and how much. Now let's consider a bit different scenario. You invite some people over to your house as before and decide to make soup, even though you know nothing about making soup. You chop (using that knife—it never gets dull), you simmer, you season, yet your soup still tastes like someone boiled a sock and sprinkled dust bunnies on the outcome (fluffy dust bunnies, though, thanks to the Handy-Dandy Dust Bunny Fluffer). As you reach frantically for the spice rack in despair, you knock it into your enormous soup bowl. After fishing the spice jars out one by one, you give the soup a final taste and, wonder of wonders, it's delicious—like a party in your mouth! As you serve it up to your guests, what emotion should you feel this time?

Not pride, not this time. You had nothing to do with how the soup came out, and your emotions will show it. A good thing happened, you did it, but you had no control over the outcome, so according to Weiner you're going to feel lucky or fortunate in this case. Now consider what happens if we alter the scenario even more. You're making your soup, the guests are outside waiting, each with a soup spoon in one hand and a hunk of bread to wipe the bowl in the other, and you can't seem to get the soup to stop tasting like dust-bunny garnished boiled socks. Your friend the gourmet chef comes in to check on what's taking so long, sees your despair, and then proceeds to add just the right spices to make the soup delicious. What emotion are you feeling now as you serve this culinary masterpiece?

You're already way ahead of me—you're feeling gratitude as you serve the soup, gratitude toward the friend who saved you. The reason you're feeling gratitude is that a good thing happened, someone else was responsible, and it was controllable—the person didn't have to do it but did anyway. If one of the guests were to compliment the soup, you'd probably immediately decline the comment and defer it to the friend who saved you, and you'd feel that it was wrong to accept the compliment without explanation.

Last one—you're making the soup, it tastes like dust-bunny flavored socks, and your friend who knows nothing about soup or cooking comes in, brushes the counter, and knocks the spice rack into the soup. When you've fished everything out, the soup is inexplicably delicious. Are you grateful to the friend now? Of course not, because the action was uncontrollable—he didn't intentionally make the soup great, and he doesn't deserve any gratitude that it accidentally turned out that way. What you feel is what you felt in the scenario where you accidentally knocked in the spice rack yourself—you feel lucky.

Put them all together, and here's the whole panoply of emotions for good outcomes:

		Controllability	
		Uncontrollable	Controllable
Locus of Causation	External	Lucky	Grateful
	Internal	Lucky	Proud

There's a symmetry here, too: When we feel pride, we expect others to feel gratitude, and when we feel gratitude, we expect others to feel pride. If we feel that someone has quite accidentally done something good for us, we don't feel gratitude toward them, and we'd deny they ought to be proud of the outcome. Likewise, when we do someone a good turn that we're not compelled to do but chose to do anyway, we feel pride and expect them to feel grateful. But if you do someone a good turn accidentally or because you had no choice, we don't feel proud, and the person we did it for doesn't feel grateful, either.

Learned Helplessness

Clearly, then, our emotions lean heavily on whether we believe we can control things or not. Dr. Martin Seligman provided even more evidence that this is the case in his formulation of what is now called "learned helplessness" (Seligman, 1973).
Learned helplessness originated in animal research, but has emerged to be one of the most significant theories of the origins of depression in humans. Let's say you have some pet lab rats. (Doesn't everybody? They make good snacks for the family dragon.) You make your rats a cage with a divider in the center

that's high enough that the rats can cross it if they really, really try, but not easily (kind of like that wall in a standard obstacle course). You mount a red light you can turn on and off on the wall of cage, high enough that it can be seen from both sides. Then you put the rats in one side of the cage. After giving the rats a few minutes to get acclimated to it, you turn on the red light. Five seconds later, you electrify the side of the cage where they're currently standing so that all the rats are getting a painful but not health-endangering shock. (Put aside, for the moment, whether we ought to be shocking innocent little rats—this is just a thought experiment, so only little thoughts of rats are suffering, not rats themselves). You've only electrified the one side, so if the rats jump the barrier they can escape the shock. Generally, that's just what they do. Rats are clever little beasts for creatures with brains the size of jelly beans, and they quickly learn to jump the barrier in this situation. In fact, in short order they learn to jump the barrier as soon as the red light goes on, before the shock comes, thus avoiding the shock entirely.

Now suppose we alter the experiment just a bit. This time, five seconds after the light comes on, we electrify the cage on both sides of the barrier, as well as the barrier itself. Now, even if the rats climb the barrier, they can't escape the shock. In fact, nothing they can do will allow them to escape the shock.

What generally happens in this situation is that the rats try a number of things. They scale the barrier between the sides of the cage, the run around their side of the cage madly, and they try to climb the walls. Eventually they give up, and settle into cowering with fear whenever the light comes on. Now let's say at this point that we change the scenario to match our initial example, electrifying only half the cage, so that now all our rats could escape by simply scaling the barrier between the two halves of the cage.

You might think the rats would learn to do so. After all, they did it easily before. But that isn't what happens. Instead, the rats continue to do nothing but cower each time the light comes on, and endure the shock when it occurs. They could escape now, but they don't learn to do so. They don't do anything. They've learned to be helpless.

Seligman pointed out that this learned helplessness was a condition that could occur in human lives as well. People are often placed in bad situations where nothing they do seems to allow them to escape or make things better. They may try different things for a period of time, but eventually they give up trying to change anything, because nothing they can think of works to free them from the bad situation. If, down the road, they suddenly have it in their power to make a difference and escape the bad situation, they may not notice, because they've given up entirely on trying. They've learned to be helpless.

Learned helplessness and depression go hand in hand. Depressed people generally suffer from learned helplessness (Seligman, Schulman, DeRubeis, & Hollon, 1999). They've often experienced a lengthy period of time where they had no power to change situations in their lives for the better, and they've finally given up trying. Then, when they're offered a chance to escape from their problems, they often refuse to take it, arguing that it won't make any difference and that their situation will never be any better regardless of what they do.

Back when I was working my way through college, I worked for a summer on the evening shift in a nursing home. Among the aides working with me that summer were several of the most unaccountably depressed people with whom I've ever had the occasion to change a bed. Their general message in every conversation we had was that life sucked, life has always sucked, and life would continue to suck into the foreseeable future. More notably, they immediately dismissed any suggestion that they could do something to make things better. For example, as we approached the Fourth of July, the scheduler came by during break to ask who wanted to work on the Fourth, pointing out we'd get time and a half if we volunteered. Being always short of money in those days (and now, for that matter), I immediately volunteered, and was added to the shift. After the scheduler had left, one of the aides asked me why I'd volunteered. "It'll put you in a higher tax bracket," she said. "You just end up with less money."

I spent the rest of the break trying to explain to her and our coworkers that this wasn't possible. In the first place, we didn't make enough money to pay any appreciable amount of income tax. In the second place, it would have taken a very large increase in income to move us to a higher bracket where our tax percentage would increase. Thirdly, even if one does go into a higher income tax bracket, only the additional money you make is taxed at that higher level, not all of your income. So it simply wasn't possible that I would end up with less money by earning more. When I wrapped up the third point, she merely shrugged at me. "You'll still end up with less," she said. "Because when you earn more, something always comes along and takes it all. Your car will break down, or you'll get a parking ticket, or you'll get sick and have to give it to the doctor. People like us never end up with more."

Now that's learned helplessness with a capital "L" and "H." My pessimistic co-worker and her colleagues were convinced that you can't get ahead in life, and as a result consistently dismissed any possible routes that might actually promise to make that happen. Like the rats cowering on their side of the barrier when escape was only a jump away, they'd learned to be helpless, and in learning to be helpless had ensured that there's no chance they would ever discover that they actually could affect the outcome after all.

There is evidence that people actually vary considerably on the degree to which they believe that they can control outcomes. Psychologists call this belief *locus of control,* (Rotter, 1966) and they believe that it has a big influence on both our mood and our behavior patterns. People who believe that they have the ability to control their own fates are said to have an *internal locus of control.* Those who do not are said to have an *external locus of control.* People with an internal locus of control take the credit and the blame for past outcomes. They're likely to be optimistic about the future and, as a result, they tend to take action. Those with an external locus of control, on the other hand, take neither credit nor blame for past outcomes. They tend to be pessimistic and they tend to be more passive, not taking action and letting whatever happens happen.

Suppose Lutwidge has an internal locus of control, and thus he believes that how he'll do on tests in his psychology class is due to actions he controls, such as studying hard. Thus he believes that the tests he's gotten good grades on turned out that way because he studied, and the tests he's done poorly on turned out that way also because he didn't study. If you were to ask him about the next test, he's apt to be optimistic, and he's apt to take action. "I'm going to do well on the next test," he'd say, "because I'm going to study all weekend." Now suppose instead that Lutwidge has an external locus of control, and thus he believes that how he'll do on tests in his psychology class is due to things not in his control, such as luck. If you were to ask him about the next test, he's apt to be pessimistic and he's apt to be passive. "I probably won't do well on the next test, either," he'd say. "And there's no point studying, because it's all luck."

What we've got here is what's called a *self-fulfilling prophecy* situation. A self-fulfilling prophecy can occur whenever we make a prediction to those very people who have it in their power to make that prediction come true. Hearing the prediction, those people are apt to engage in behavior that makes the prediction happen because they believe that it is going to. For example, suppose a very famous market guru announces to all his followers that a particular stock is going to rise spectacularly in the next week. His followers immediately go out and buy the stock, causing it to rise in price because of the demand that they themselves created. Our market guru has just committed a self-fulfilling prophesy, putting into motion what he predicted by making the prediction itself to those who were likely to make his prediction happen, the buyers of stock.

What does this have to do with locus of control? Your locus of control creates the ultimate in self-fulfilling prophesies. If you have an internal locus of control, you'll be optimistic, and you'll take action. In taking action, you're more likely to succeed than if you had not taken action, so the very belief that you can accomplish something leads to your accomplishing something. If you have an external locus of control, you'll be pessimistic about the future, so you probably won't take action. Not taking action makes it much more likely you'll fail, again meaning that your very belief leads to the outcome. Henry Ford never studied locus of control, but by his quote at the start of the chapter it's clear he understood self-fulfilling prophecies of this nature.

Cognitive and behavioral therapists address this issue directly when they work with depressed patients. One of the big goals in cognitive/behavioral therapy is to inspire the patient to actually make plans to get out and do things, and then follow through on those plans. Once they start trying to do things, the patients actually succeed at some of them, and with any luck they'll then try more and more things, with each success trying more and more things until they overcome their learned helplessness

What therapists are trying to do here is raise people's sense of self-efficacy, or our belief that we can do things. As we increase our belief that we can effectively do things, we are more likely to actually try to improve our situations. At least some of the time we'll be successful, and that will raise our sense of self-efficacy, which in turn will lead us to try to do even more.

Albert Bandura, who we discussed before when we brought up reciprocal control in *Chapter 4: Teaching Old Dogs New Tricks*, created a controversy some years back with a simple proposal. He was addressing the issue of how psychology has many, many different models of therapy, ranging from Freudian, Adlerian, and Jungian psychodynamics through Rogers' Client Centered Therapy all the way to Behaviorism and Behavior Modification, and finally to Cognitive Therapy. Each of these therapies has its own adherents and its own promoters. All of these therapies appear to help at least some people to a greater or lesser degree. Yet they all go about it very differently, and sometimes they contradict each other in terms of what they suggest patients must do. For example, psychodynamic therapists argue we must unearth and wallow in our anxieties, whereas cognitive therapy often suggests we simply need to bury them more effectively. You really couldn't get any more contradictory advice. Yet, patients treated with both traditions have shown improvement, so both therapies work. Bandura suggested that the reason both work is because it doesn't really matter which the patient does—all that really matters is that the patient thinks that the therapy will make him or her function better. We're raising the patient's sense of self-efficacy, thus encouraging him or her to take action. It doesn't really matter, Bandura argues, whether the patient is told to dig out his anxieties and wallow in them or bury them, as much as it matters that the patient believes that whichever one he's doing will make a difference in his or her life (Bandura, 1977).

What Makes Us Laugh?

Which brings us to another way that humans deal with anxiety and worry and accentuate the positive in life. We use humor. Humans laugh, joke, and poke fun at things, even very serious things. It's truly astonishing how, following any man-made or natural disaster or any horrifying event, jokes dealing with that catastrophe or disaster will be circulating within hours, spreading across the entire country within days. What are some of the bases of laughter, why do we do it, and what makes some events funny and some very similar events frightening?

Let's consider a scenario for a moment. A group of hunter-gatherer humans from millennia ago approach a water hole after a long hunting expedition just as dusk is settling in. They're toting the things they've gathered and hunted, and they're moving cautiously, because the savannah is a dangerous place. As they near the water hole, peering cautiously into the gloom, they start to realize that something's different from when they were last here—there are shadows there that don't match the familiar memories of this particular place, and they appear to be moving. The fact that there are shadows that weren't there before is an incongruity, and the fact that they're too vague to make out means our hunter-gatherer heroes can't yet resolve the incongruity.

Unresolvable incongruity triggers an uncomfortable state of arousal in our hominid host. The hackles start standing up on the backs of necks, hearts beat faster, crawly butterfly feelings appear in stomachs, and everyone enters a higher state of awareness.

Inching closely merely increases the incongruity—there's definitely something there, a bunch of somethings, and they're moving, but the vague visual sensations and sounds that are filtering through to the troupe can't be matched to any memories. The longer this goes on, the more unpleasant mental arousal takes place in our approaching tribe.

Suddenly, with whooping cries, the confusing, disturbing shadows break loose and charge right at our intrepid group. Just before our brave little crew can launch their tightly-gripped spears or turn and flee, the shadows clarify and become a troupe of small apes, fleeing our approaching hunter-gatherer troupe. The arousal of our hominids, which had peaked just seconds before when it appeared they were under attack, collapses into massive relief as they resolve the true nature of the incongruous shadows into the category of harmless things.

What very likely will happen next is that our hunter gatherers will dissolve into gales of laughter, slapping various other tribe members on the back and saying things (in their own languages, of course, which were undoubtedly as rich and diverse as our own) like "Boy, you should have seen your face," and "I thought you were going to leave your big, fat, dirty footprints on my back running over me trying to get away."

In this example, our hunter-gatherers have a good long laugh, and may retell the story again for years, laughing each time over how frightened they were for a minute. But the laughter itself was born of arousal due to anxiety, and the anxiety was due to incongruity. There was something in the world that didn't fit, and that lack of fit bothered our Paleozoic protagonists. Incongruity raises anxiety, and there's great survival value in that. When things don't fit or aren't the same as you remember them, it's best to be cautious of them, poised on the knife edge of fight or flight until you can be sure that the incongruity is harmless.

Not surprisingly given its survival value, we're not the only species that doesn't like things that don't fit. I grew up on a Southeastern Iowa dairy farm, near a small town with the improbable but adorable name of Columbus Junction. My parents milked cows every morning and every night of every day, and my brothers and I helped out by feeding the calves, cleaning equipment and barns once milking was done, filling hay mangers for the cows, and more other little tasks than I now care to remember. One summer morning we milked the cows as usual, turned them out to pasture, then spent the day building a new feed bin on the side of the barn where the cows normally entered, finishing the job just about the evening milking time. As a result of our work, the side of the barn next to the barn door now had a new access door in it, and the boards above and below that access door had been replaced with new wood that had not yet been painted white like the rest of the barn. As the cows mosied up the barnyard, ready for their evening corn and the relief of being milked (a good Holstein cow might produce 5 gallons of milk in one milking. A gallon of milk, like a gallon of water, weighs 8 lbs, so they're carrying 40 extra pounds in their udders by milking time—you'd be relieved, too).

Anyway, the cows ambled up the barnyard in their usual loose formation, with the dominant cows leading and the submissive cows following, drifting toward the barn door, when suddenly the lead cow spotted the new, unpainted wood patch and new door on the side of the barn. She stopped dead, planted both feet apart from each other, stretched her neck out, and stared at the barn wall with what could only be called deep suspicion. Behind her, the other cows stopped dead and planted their feet, also stretching their necks out to look at this new, incongruous thing. Behind them, the rest of the herd stopped dead as well, watching the cows in front of them.

The whole group stood there, frozen, for an extended period of time, eyes wide, while my brothers and I gently encouraged them from the sides and behind, talking soothingly, urging them forward. Finally, the lead cow, an intrepid old girl with more courage than most of the others, took a step closer, then another, then another, eyeing the new patch suspiciously on her approach until she could final duck her head into the barn door, leaving the disturbing woodwork behind with a swish of her tail and what could only be called bovine relief. One by one the other cows followed, each needing some urging to pass the spot with the new woodwork. It was a delicate situation for a bit, though—all it would have taken was a sudden loud noise or something making a sudden movement toward the cows in front and the whole mass would have turned tail and charged down the barnyard.

You can see the survival value in herd animals and social animals, like cows and humans, feeling a sense of anxiety whenever a situation doesn't match our memories or doesn't make sense to us. Such situations are more likely to be dangerous than the familiar things that we can make sense out of. It's just plain wise to be cautious with things don't jive with how you remember them. But there's a big difference between the cows in this example and our hunter-gatherer humans in the previous one. None of the cows laughed when the situation was found to be harmless—trust me, I was there, and none of them so much as cracked a smile. Cows don't release the tension of arousal by laughter when they resolve an incongruous situation. They appear to simply calm back down again, and sometimes slowly at that, remaining on edge for some time afterward.

So humans are and aren't like cows. Like cows, when incongruity is encountered, we also feel heightened mental arousal. If that arousal continues to rise, it may culminate as fear or terror. But humans laugh when their anxiety is turns out to be groundless, bleeding off the arousal quickly into pleasurable feelings. The greater the incongruity and the more arousal it triggers before resolution, the more laughter will result. The greatest laughter is going to occur if we resolve the incongruity satisfactorily just as it's reaching a peak. But that's also when the greatest risk of fright will occur. Thus, there is often a paper-thin line that divides uproarious laughter and abject fear.

You have to be careful of this in haunted house situations, scary stories, or even just the grand old human game of hiding somewhere and jumping out at people, especially when the little ones are involved. Mostly, you'll get laughter from these activities, as the fear of the person resolves into understanding that what had at first appeared a threat is harmless. But sometimes you'll create too much arousal before the resolution of harmlessness, so much that you trigger fear instead. Then you'll find yourself trying to comfort the sobbing, frightened target of your little joke and feeling like a big jerk.

I made that mistake with my older son once. We were riding along on our way to school when a song started playing on the radio, a great little piece by Rose and the Arrangement entitled *The Cockroach that Ate Cincinnati*, (later made into a B movie). I made the mistake of waiting for the initial buildup of the song, then suddenly, along with the lead singer, shouting at my then 8-year-old son, "Aha! Don't touch that dial!" Not one of my better moves—he recoiled in terror and then burst into tears. (Hey, don't look at me like that—it's not like none of you have ever hidden and jumped out at someone only to get the same reaction. Besides, he turned out okay. (Well, sort of okay. He's an avid player of an obscure game called underwater hockey, so I can't argue that he's not just a little bit different.)

The bottom line is this: things that don't make sense or are incongruous make us anxious, and that anxiety may bleed off into laughter or rise into terror, depending on the circumstances. This is one of the reasons why absolutely nobody, ever, has as much fun as a 2-year-old. Two-year-olds are constantly laughing at everything, everywhere. They're the most tickled people on Earth. One of the reasons two-year-olds laugh so much, though, is for the same reason that we often laugh, because things that are confusing or incongruous breed tension and arousal, and this arousal can be bled off in laughter. In the case of us older people, this often happens because we've resolved the incongruity that caused the anxiety to start with, but this isn't absolutely necessary—we'll often laugh just because things are incongruous, but don't appear threatening. Moderate amounts of incongruity alone will trigger laughter at times at any age, whether the incongruity is resolved or not. But it's extreme with two-year-olds. They understand almost nothing, everything is new and many things are incongruous to them, and the net result is that THEY LAUGH ALL THE TIME!

This is not an exaggeration. Two-year olds laugh constantly. And they'll laugh at the same thing, repeated over and over—in fact, the more times you repeat the thing, the louder and longer they'll laugh. Make an unexpected noise, and they'll want you to make it again and again. Trip and fall, and you'll not only have the indignity of picking your old bones off the ground again, but you get to do it while your toddler busts a gut and shrieks at you, "Do it again! Do it again!"

There's one final aspect of children and laughter that you have to understand, too, especially if you're going to interact with children. As we've already discussed, because of that fine line between terror and uproarious laughter, children often cry in fear when we expect them to laugh. The opposite also occurs—they laugh when we expected them to show fear. Many, many children, when they have been caught at some wrongdoing and are being dressed down by adults or threatened with dire punishment, have outraged those adults by laughing. The laughter here often infuriates the adult, yet it's not necessarily a sign the child is being defiant or, worse, is a budding antisocial personality. It may be that he or she has merely triggered the wrong anxiety response. While poised on the knife edge between terror and laughter, the child has teetered down the wrong side.

Are we the only species that laughs? There are quite a few animals that make noises somewhat like laughter. Hyenas, for example, have a haunting call that sounds like hysterical human laughter, but this is simply their form of barking, and thus not akin to the human noise that sounds so similar. The same could be said about the kookaburra, a species of Australian kingfisher that has a call that resembles the maniacal laughter of the stereotypic mad scientist in a "B" movie (with a title such as *The Cockroach that Ate Cincinnati*). And birds that mimic, such as parakeets, parrots, and cockatiels sometimes do a good imitation of human laughter, but they're not the least bit tickled when they do it, any more than when they "talk," or ring like a telephone.

What animals laugh in the human way? That is, what animals laugh when physically tickled, when faced with incongruous situations that turn out to be harmless, and in social interactions? In examining laughter triggered by tickling, Dr. Marina Davila Ross discovered that there is great similarity between the vocal patterns of human laughter and that of great apes, including orangutans, gorillas, bonobos, and chimpanzees (Davila Ross, 2009). Orangutans also appear to laugh at incongruity, but, according to Davila Ross, don't use laughter in social situations. That leaves gorillas, bonobos, and chimpanzees, all of whom appear to laugh in the human fashion. Davila-Ross argues that this indicates that social laughter, rather than laughter that arises for arousal, is a relatively new inclination, arising after the orangutans split off from the other ape groups. For these relatively recent primates, laughter serves multiple purposes, some of them social. Laughter is contagious and reduces group tensions, and in doing so reduces the likelihood of in-group violence. Get the angry guy to laugh, and maybe you'll reducc his tension enough he won't seriously injure or kill you. Laughter is also highly rewarding, in that it bleeds off our tensions; one of the reasons we make jokes about many of the awful things in life. It ties people and groups together. When others make us laugh, we associate that enjoyment with the persons who triggered those good feelings, thus enhancing group ties.

Humor also, as Aristotle pointed out, allows us to feel superior to others by characterizing them as buffoons or as idiots who do incongruous and idiotic things that we're too smart to do (Sachs, 2008). There are all sorts of regional jokes, for example, where people make fun of people who are their rivals for athletic contests or for more serious stakes. Lawyer jokes are examples of this as well, enabling the person telling the joke to strike back at a group that is often feared, and in doing so feel superior.

We laugh at incongruous things, but we laugh harder if that incongruity suddenly makes sense, as was the case in the example of our hunter/gatherer hominids above who encountered the apes fleeing the watering hole. Many jokes are structured to create such a situation. Such jokes are called incongruity/resolution jokes, in that they deliberately set up an incongruous situation, make us wonder how it's going to turn out, and then just as our tension has peaked quickly provide the information that allows us to resolve the joke (McGhee, & Goldstein, 1983).

Consider, for example, this little gem from the business world:

A group of managers from a big company decided to have a managers' picnic. As part of the picnic they set up all sorts of rides for the families, food stands, entertainment, and so on. The highlight of the picnic was a hot-air balloon on a tether—the managers were allowed to, one by one, get in the basket of the balloon, turn up the burner, and soar up into the air to the end of the rope. After their turn was up, they were to turn off the burner under the balloon and drift back down so the next person could ride. As luck would have it, though, fog started rolling in as the last manager went up, so he was soon unable to see the ground. Deciding he might as well come down, he went to shut off the burner, but forgetting how to do it, he accidentally triggered the release for the tether rope instead, and off he floated into the fog. Realizing the ocean was out there somewhere, but fearful of trees and power lines, our wayward manager started gradually turning the burner down (he'd finally found the controls), and staring down into the fog trying to see land. He kept slipping lower and lower, and finally he came out of the fog and realized that he appeared to be hovering over a small hill and that, even more promising, a man was on top the hill looking up at him.

Leaning over the side of the balloon, he called down, "WHERE AM I?"

The man on the ground considered a minute, then shouted up, "YOU ARE IN A HOT AIR BALLOON ABOUT 20 FEET ABOVE THE GROUND."

The manager in the balloon considered a moment, then nodded in satisfaction. "AH," he called down. "YOU'RE AN ENGINEER!"

The man on the ground looked surprised. "HOW DID YOU KNOW I WAS AN ENGINEER?" he called back.

"BECAUSE YOUR ANSWER, ALTHOUGH TECHNICALLY CORRECT, WAS COMPLETELY USELESS FOR ALL PRACTICAL PURPOSES," the manager called back down.

The man on the ground thought for a minute, then his own eyes lit up. "I GET IT!" he shouted up at the balloon. "YOU'RE A COMPANY MANAGER!"

"WHY YES," the manager shouted back. "HOW DID YOU KNOW?"

"BECAUSE," the ground-bound engineer shouted back. "YOU DON'T KNOW WHERE YOU ARE. YOU DON'T KNOW WHERE YOU'RE GOING. YET YOU MANAGED TO BLAME IT ALL ON ME!"

Now, assuming you find that humorous, let's take a look at how that happened (If you didn't find it humorous, there's no helping you). As the set-up to the joke is related, the listener follows along with the story, meanwhile trying to anticipate where it's going, with tension building during this time. When the joke teller gets to the part where our manager first suggests that the person on the ground is an engineer, the listener reaches a new height of arousal, because he or she is puzzled for a moment. It isn't immediately obvious how the manager jumped to the conclusion that the man on the ground is an engineer. The tension of being unable to see the connection reaches its highest level so far. The manager's reply, in the form of the punch line, instantaneously allows us to make sense of it all. The listener suddenly recognizes the line of reasoning. "Oh, of course. The stereotype of engineers is that they're very precise but not realistic or focused on real-world solutions. This fellow's answer was like that, so the manager knew he was an engineer." Suddenly it all makes sense, the tension resolves almost instantaneously, and the listener laughs (admit it, you did laugh. Or at least chuckle appreciatively.)

This particular joke, though, has a second part. When the joke doesn't stop, but instead goes on, tension starts rising in the listener again, as he or she wonders where the joke teller is going with it now. The joke-teller goes into the second setup immediately, with the engineer's identification of the man in the balloon as a manager. This time more tension is raised, because the listener senses that this should also resolve like the first one, with a stereotypic quality of managers. With luck, though, the resolution isn't immediately obvious, so the joke teller times it just right, then hits the listener with the punch line, allowing the listener to resolve the joke by suddenly realizing it makes sense because managers are notorious for screwing things up and blaming the engineers, and the even higher tension of the second incongruity resolves, bringing gales of uncontrollable laughter, more this time because of the recognition not just of how the punch line resolves the incongruity, but how the two incongruities are related.

Incongruity/resolution jokes tend to be preferred by older children and adults over jokes that involve incongruity alone. Younger children, though, aren't so picky. For one thing, children under 6 understand so little about the world that they often aren't able to resolve incongruous situations, so they simply develop tension due to the incongruity set up in the joke, then release it in laughter. When they tell jokes of their own, they seldom have punch lines, at least not punch lines that resolve the incongruity, and they don't need them. Often, younger children are laughing at an entirely different aspect of the jokes they hear and tell than older children and adults are. (Shultz, 1972).

Take this example of a fairly simple juvenile joke, adapted from Shultz.

A man walks into a pizza parlor. He tells the man behind the counter, "Give me a large pepperoni pizza." The man behind the counter says, "Yes, sir! And would you like that cut into eight pieces, or twelve?" "Eight," the man replies. "I could never eat twelve pieces of pizza."

A five-year-old might get great pleasure in telling such a joke, and might laugh as uproariously as everyone else at the punch line. But while older people would be laughing because the man clearly picked eight because he thinks that if you cut a pizza into twelve pieces that makes for more pizza, our five-year old, if asked why it was funny, is likely to say that it's funny because the man's going to eat a whole pizza by himself.

In fact, when they do try to tell jokes, it's common for children under six or seven to completely mangle the punch line and laugh just as hard anyway, totally unaware that it was even part of why the joke was funny. One little boy, for example, when asked to tell a joke, related an old chestnut of a joke in which a woman opens her refrigerator and finds a squirrel stretched out on the shelf. The woman says, “What are you doing in my refrigerator?” Now at this point, the squirrel is supposed to say, “Isn’t this a Westinghouse?” and when the woman agrees that it is, he’s supposed to say, “Well, I’m westing!” But when the boy told the joke, he had the squirrel say, “Isn’t this a refrigerator? Well, I’m taking a nap!” At that point, the boy dissolved into uncontrollable laughter. When asked later, after he’d stopped laughing, why the joke was funny, he said it was because the squirrel was sleeping in the refrigerator. The incongruity was enough—he didn’t need the resolution that adults count on in the form of the punch line.

One of the big factors in just how much laughter we can trigger in telling a joke or a funny story is what comedians call *timing.* It simply refers to monitoring the audience closely and making sure that we move the story along at the right speed to build tension steadily on our way to the punch line, then triggering the punch line when tension reaches its peak. As any comedian could tell you, it’s a tough thing to do. You have to slow down for drunk audiences and spell the details out more for them, but if you take too long, the tension will bleed off again before you can spring the punch line, and the results won’t be as satisfactory, either.

As comedians age, like all of us, their vision becomes less good, especially in dim conditions like those found in nightclubs and bars, and their hearing diminishes sharply. It gets harder and harder to read audiences and adjust the pace of the joke and the timing of the punch lines. They spring the punch line too soon or too late, they explain too much or too little, and they become a caricature of their former selves. Comedians call this losing their timing, and it usually constitutes the death knell for their careers.

The bottom line is that how incongruous things are and whether we can resolve that incongruity determines whether we’ll sigh, groan, laugh, or flee in terror. In fact, a great deal of things in our lives, and our enjoyment of life itself, depends upon how we look at things. Whether we laugh or experience heart-thumping terror, whether we fear the future or embrace it, whether we take action or sit and mope, whether you feel helpless or empowered, whether you're angry or pitying or ashamed or feel guilty, whether you feel proud or grateful or lucky, all these depend upon how you look at things. It's the final message I want to pass along to you in this current volume. You can choose how you look at things. To that degree, you have it in your power to make your own world, and to seize life by the lapels and give it a good shake. Me, I plan to accentuate the positive and eliminate the negative. Mr. In-Between is on his own.

References:

Bandura, A. (1997). *Self-efficacy: The exercise of control.* New York: Worth.

Davila Ross, Marina. (2009). Reconstructing the Evolution of Laughter in Great Apes and Humans, *Current Biology*, *19*, 1106-1111.

McGhee, P. E., & Goldstein, J. H., eds. (1983). *Handbook of humor research: Basic issues, Vol. 1.* New York: Springer-Verlag.

Rotter, J. (1966). Generalized expectancies for internal versus external control of reinforcement. *Psychological Monographs*, *80* (1).

Sachs, J. (2008). *Nicomachean Ethic, Aristotle. Newburyport, MA: Focus.*

Shultz, T. R. (1972). The role of incongruity and resolution in children's appreciation of cartoon humor. *Journal of Experimental Child Psychology*, 13 (3), pp. 456-477.

Seligman, M. E. P., & Johnston, J. C. (1973). A cognitive theory of avoidance learning. In F. J. McGuigan & D. B. Lumsden (Eds.), *Contemporary approaches to conditioning and learning*. Washington, D. C.: Winston.

Seligman, M. E. P., Schulman, P., DeRubeis, R. J., & Hollon, S. D. (1999). The prevention of depression and anxiety. *Prevention and Treatment, 2*.

Weiner, B. (1985). A attributional theory of achievement motivation and emotion. Psychological Review, *92*, 548-573.

ABOUT THE AUTHOR

Dr. Dean Richards grew up on a dairy farm near Columbus Junction, Iowa, but he left cold, damp winters and hot, humid summers behind forever after finishing graduate school. He now lives in Los Angeles with his lovely wife, Dr. Andrea Richards, enjoying periodic visits from their now grown children, generating almost all his own electricity from clean, silent solar panels, raising backyard tomatoes, working on the next volume of this series, and teaching psychology online as well as on site for a myriad of universities. He hopes you have enjoyed this volume of essays on psychology, and if so, he invites you to read the other volume in this series, *Psychology in Plain English*, (provided you have not done so already). Both this volume and that one are available in paperback and for Kindle and Kindle Reader Apps on Amazon.com.

Dean enjoys hearing from readers, and appreciates online reviewers. If you'd like to contact him, you can do so at this email address:

deanrichardsbooks@gmail.com

Reviews can be posted for this volume on its web page on Amazon.com. The Amazon Kindle app for smartphones, tablets, and desktop computers can also be downloaded from Amazon.com. If you liked this book, please recommend it to a friend, or order a copy through Amazon to give as a lovely gift! Heck, order 10—shipping costs are much cheaper if you do!

CPSIA information can be obtained at www.ICGtesting.com
Printed in the USA
LVOW071958271212

313486LV00029B/1367/P

9 781479 168415